Authentic and relatable, this bo[...] take an honest look at themselv[...] with wit, humor, and vulnerab[...], [...] insecurity, rejection, and uncertainty while pointing girls to the truth of who they really are. As God's loved and forgiven daughters, they have an unchanging identity and value in Christ that allows them to shine! I will be giving a copy to each girl in my youth group.

—Jessica Bordeleau, MAR, LCMS Lutheran Youth Fellowship coordinator, freelance author, media producer, and educational resource developer

Communicating clearly with preteens and teens is one of the most difficult tasks to accomplish. In *Shine: Sparkling with God's Love*, Christina Hergenrader enables conversation and discussion with finesse. She challenges young women to boldly shine with the love of Christ and also rest in His radiance when life seems to overwhelm. I could almost see the sparkle of her pen strokes as her words effervescently and lightheartedly brought order and intention to the many concerns our girls are facing today. Captivating and easy to follow, *Shine* is a wonderfully pertinent biblical study for tween and teen girls everywhere.

—Heather Ruesch, life-issues speaker
and author of *Sexuality Mentality*

Shine

SPARKLING WITH GOD'S LOVE

Christina Hergenrader

CONCORDIA PUBLISHING HOUSE · SAINT LOUIS

This book is for my goddaughters:
Kate Leimbach, Lydia Ward, Bella Axcell,
Lanie Ward, and Emmy Hergenrader.
Shine brightly, beautiful girls.
Jesus loves you.
And that means you are enough.

Founded in 1869 as the publishing arm of The Lutheran
Church—Missouri Synod, Concordia Publishing House gives
all glory to God for the blessing of 150 years of opportunities
to provide resources that are faithful to the Holy Scriptures
and the Lutheran Confessions.

Published by Concordia Publishing House
3558 S. Jefferson Ave., St. Louis, MO 63118–3968
1-800-325-3040 • cph.org

Unless otherwise indicated, Scripture quotations are from the ESV® Bible (The Holy Bible, English Standard Version®), copy-
right © 2001 by Crossway, a publishing ministry of Good News Publishers. Used by permission. All rights reserved.

Manufactured in the United States of America

1   2   3   4   5   6   7   8   9   10   28   27   26   25   24   23   22   21   20   19

TABLE OF CONTENTS

Carter ~
Surf on!

Christin
Hoyfedler

Dear Beautiful Readers . . .

Can we talk about pressure?

The pressure to stay connected all the time . . . to always be your cutest, funniest self . . . to try all the activities . . . to keep up with the constant schedule . . . to take advantage of every minute, each opportunity, all the advantages . . .

Pressure can destroy. The force of it exposes weaknesses and creates cracks. Yes, this happens in science, but it also happens with you, dear girl. Too much pressure, and you'll find yourself wondering who you are and how you can escape the stress of your very own life.

The truth is that pressure is as much a part of our modern lives as texting and Amazon Prime. Yet it's hard to know how to deal with the weight of so many expectations. On your busiest days, it might feel like your cracks are showing. You want answers, but you don't know who to ask because everyone around you is under the same stresses and strain.

Plus, you don't want to just survive the pressure. You want to thrive.

Here's the good news: you can do exactly that. Because sometimes pressure doesn't form cracks—it forms diamonds. What will pressure do to you? That depends on what's inside you.

Are you filled up with the richer nutrients from your heavenly Father? Do you trust all the ways He takes care of you? Do you believe that you are already enough, just because you are so loved?

In these pages, you'll discover the very excellent news that God has chosen you to shine. And you can, because as a daughter of your heavenly Father, you do have everything you need.

Your Father loves you so much. He wants you to reflect that love like billions of pieces of brilliant, bright glitter.

Let's look at how you can do exactly that.

Shine on with God's love!
Christina Hergenrader

Rise and Shine

*Arise, shine, for your light has come, and the
glory of the LORD has risen upon you.*

—ISAIAH 60:1

Imagine these thrilling moments:

✳ The surprise of five hundred "likes" on your Instagram
post.

✳ The satisfaction of getting your eyeliner exactly right the
first time.

✳ A card from your mom telling you that you are the
sweetest daughter.

✳ Finding a prom dress that's 50 percent off and fits
perfectly.

✳ Overhearing your dad telling his friends what a "super-
star student" you are.

✳ Finding a forgotten twenty-dollar bill in your pocket.

All of these moments zing delight through your ho-hum day.
These instants are filled with warm glow, with adrenaline, with
Christmas-morning excitement.

This is a tiny bit of what God's people experienced when the
Old Testament prophet Isaiah said these words: "Arise, shine, for
your light has come, and the glory of the LORD has risen upon you"
(Isaiah 60:1).

You see, God's people had been in a bad place. They were slaves. Their king was literally crazy, and they were very hungry. To say life felt hopeless would be an understatement.

Maybe the situation was even worse because God had warned His people that their sin was leading them to this kind of darkness. But over and over, they kept sinning and worshiping false gods. They kept repeating the same sins God had said would hurt them. (Imagine how your mom feels when you have blown off her warnings about ignoring your homework. You've been telling her, "I am handling it!" and now you're on academic probation. The angry emoji does not do justice to the smoke coming out of her ears.)

But God didn't leave His people stranded in their own bad decisions. He promised to send His Son to die for their sins. God gave His wayward people an exit plan from all their dark sin.

This was the promise in Isaiah 60, that the glory of the Lord had come.

The promise of Isaiah—of God's brilliant, blinding glory—is our promise too. Jesus has come for us, and He is coming again. Because of that, you have the light of Christ inside you.

You are still living in a dark world of sin, but you know that you belong to something richer, something better.

In this section, we'll look at some of the darkness in our world: toxic friendships, the terror of a school shooting, the crush who lives up to his name, and the problems with social media. We'll also talk about how you can handle the pressure of all these things to become a floodlight of God's love.

Shine on, dear girl. God has given you His best joy, the true delight for your heart.

And you get to shine it to the world.

How to Keep Shining God's Light

(And Six Friends Who Want to Put It Out)

This is an (incomplete) list of those toxic friendships that can cause so much darkness in your world. If you recognize some of these characters from your actual life, read on to discover how you can rely on God to help you share His love with friends who need it.

1. THE GOSSIP

Of course you're aware that this particular friend has some issues. She loves telling you all the dirt—the problem is that most of it is so mean. Also, she can't be entirely sure any of it is actually true.

The real problem is that her stories are so interesting. How else would you learn that your geometry teacher is actually gay and your former best friend is probably anorexic and your crush cheats to pass biology?

It feels a little cheap to know all this about people. But also super interesting. And if you're being honest, it kind of makes you feel better about yourself to know everyone else has these big secrets.

Except all this comes crashing down when you find out that your gossiping friend is actually telling your secrets too. She's on text threads separate from you, and when you're scrolling through her phone, you find the secret you told her about your parents not speaking to each other.

So, what to do now? You could spread some lovely stories about your gossiping friend—particularly about how she sleeps with her lights on because she has a strange fear of wolves.

Revenge storytelling about this particular friend would feel so very sweet.

But you realize that gossiping can do serious damage (and besides, there's a whole commandment about it).

You will need God's help to forgive. Ask Him to help you deal with your anger, for discernment in confronting her, and for the wisdom not to get wrapped up in her gossip in the first place. Ask God for an exit strategy the next time she starts to spill the tea so you can tell her that you don't want to be part of it.

2. THE CONTROL FREAK

True, this friend does like to be in charge. But she's also the very best at organizing you and your life.

With a friend like this, you always know what's expected of you. Usually that is that you should do what she tells you to do: *Call me at exactly eight o'clock. . . . Meet me for lunch right in our spot and right on time. . . . Remember that I hate when you bring turkey sandwiches because the smell makes me nauseous.*

Life gets a bit tricky with your friend when you don't follow the rules exactly as she would like. For example, the time you went totally off script and brought other friends to your lunch table. This became the moment when you realized you should not rock her boat. EVVVERRRRR!

What can you do, except try to tell her your side of the story?

("I'm sorry I wore my hair down when you like for us to match on Fridays. . . . Please forgive me for not laughing hard enough when you were trying to tell the joke to your crush. I really wasn't trying to annoy you.")

But then, also use this as an excellent chance to take a good look at yourself and remember that you can be friends with the kind of girl who needs the world to operate on her schedule—but without letting her take your entire identity from you. You, dear one, should never be a prop in her incredibly organized life.

This will take some work, so go back to the Lord, back to who He said you were when He claimed you in your Baptism, back to

His Word. Remember your heavenly Father's promise that He has adopted you as His daughter exactly as you are.

3. THE USER

This is nice—a new friend. She appears overnight as The One Who Is Suddenly There All the Time.

Where, oh where, has this friend been all your life?

She really "gets" you. Suddenly she's calling you, just when you've had the worst day. She's inviting you to get Starbucks with her and texting you really funny memes, and she truly seems to care about your weird love of synchronized gymnastics videos on YouTube.

Until it all becomes clear. And once you see the REAL REASON she's been the very best friend, you can't believe you ever believed she was genuine. It's your brother she's really trying to get to know better—as in, get to know him as his new girlfriend.

Or she's looking at your new car and is so ready for you to become her own personal Uber driver. Ah, now you see.

Or maybe she heard about how your uncle works for the ticket sales group for *Hamilton*, and now you know why this new "friend" has not left your side until the show comes to town.

But maybe you don't have to react with the same self-centeredness. Perhaps you can tap into a kinder, more balanced approach to friendship and talk to her about how you really hope the two of you can stay friends long after your brother announces he would never date one of his little sister's friends.

Try it and see where it goes. If you're meant to become the kind of friends who stick together, that will probably become obvious. If not, you might be better investing a little more in friends who will be by your side all the time—not just when they need a favor.

4. THE SUPER-INSECURE FRIEND

She is on the swim team with you, and you spend hours every week at the pool, pulling swim caps over each other's hair and talking about your split times.

But really, you end up spending lots of the practices assuring her that she looks just fine in her bathing suit, that she does NOT in fact swim like a bloated sea turtle, and that it is *ridiculous* to believe that the coach hates her.

Total honesty? You kind of love that you can make her feel so much better about herself. You've actually become pretty good at talking her out of her insecurity. You can pep-talk her into the pool every single day. It works so well that she seems to have become a tiny bit dependent on you.

(Okay, actually a lot dependent. Like you overheard her telling her mom that you're like HER SAVIOR. And that was just a little weird. Actually, a little nice because that sounds like she will probably always like you. But mostly weird.)

It also gets to be exhausting to always be the wind beneath someone else's wings. For just one day, you would like to NOT be a personal cheerleader.

Plus, you are a little worried about your friend. It seems like a pretty desperate place to be to need another person this much. She really doesn't believe anything good about herself.

Maybe you could share a little about Jesus with her—since He is her actual Savior. He won't exactly be there to tell her that it's okay if she's the slowest at backstroke.

Or actually, maybe He will be there. Because you know the power of prayer, and the Bible does say that the Lord is right there with us when we're scared (Psalm 34:18).

So, it's probably worth a try to share all this with her. You might lose your job as SAVIOR TO THE INSECURE . . . but that's probably better anyway.

5. THE FRIEND WHO SAYS SHE LOVES JESUS (BUT DOESN'T SEEM TO)

What a strange friend this one is.

She's the lead singer of the praise band, the one who argues against abortion in the schoolwide assembly, and the girl who quotes Bible verses to the kids who vape in the bathroom.

You want to really like her, and you totally admire her confidence, but sometimes she isn't very nice.

At first, you thought all the praying for sinners around the flagpole and going to church three times a week would be an inspiration for you. But this friend is actually kind of hurtful to anyone who doesn't meet her standards. Also, lots of days it seems like it's very important for her to keep everyone's focus on her. That's not right. Shouldn't the focus be on God?

She might be your Pharisee friend.

Remember the Pharisees in the Bible? This was pretty much their deal too. Big, grand shows of religion—then cruelty to real, actual people. They loved to prove how holy they were, but they were not so hot on pretty much everything that Jesus was saying and doing (i.e., "Love God," "Love your neighbor," "Forgive," "Show grace").

So, your gut feeling on this one was right. Your modern-day Pharisee friend needs to see what God is all about. God never tells us that we are winning at Christianity when we obey His rules perfectly. In fact, He tells us the opposite. Part of living as a Christian includes how you treat those who have the least to offer; you know, the ones who are usually invisible to everyone else (James 1:27).

So, yes, your friend who is making a big show of praying for sinners probably needs prayer herself. Ask God to show her that worshiping Him looks much more like spreading the news through hot meals for the homeless than insulting the atheists. Ask Jesus to help you lead by example and love everyone.

6. THE ANGRY FRIEND

It's not entirely clear what she's so mad about, really.

This is your friend who has a chip on her shoulder roughly the size of every person who has ever let her down.

She remains ready for anyone else to let her down—specifically you. Even though you really don't want to disappoint her, she takes it all very personally when she gets the idea that you might be a tiny bit less than loyal to her. (For example, the time when you told her that you didn't really like the same band she does and she was SO MAD because you were saying you didn't like her. Wait. What?)

There's also the constant problem of her deciding she doesn't like whole groups of people. (For example, the workers at the pet shelter—who doesn't like people who take care of homeless puppies? And she is convinced the old guy at the smoothie place hates kids. Really, he probably doesn't like how you and your friends never tip, but whatever.)

With friends like this who are angry or bitter or negative, ask God to help you keep your own identity. He might even decide to heal your friend's deep anger issues. Or maybe not. Just remember that *she* might have major issues with the cafeteria workers, but you can still smile at them as they hand you a tray of meat loaf.

GOD'S SILVER (GLITTER) LINING

Okay, you're old enough to realize that there is no perfect friend. Seriously. Movies and books are filled with these instant friends who look nothing like the people who go to your school.

From what you've probably discovered, friends are actual humans—selfish, insecure, trying really hard, and also working to figure out how to do a bit better. There will be lots of ups and downs with friends. I'm sure you have already learned this the hard way.

But here's the good news: God can—and will—work in the middle of all these relationships. To be clear, Jesus hung out with a crazy crew of sinners. Consider this: one of His friends decided to turn Him over to His enemies. This was Jesus' actual life, and yet, He never sinned. He just kept showing His friends that there was a better way.

Through all of your friendships, keep your eyes on Jesus' perfect standard. You'll see so many examples of how to love your friends well—even when one of you is off the rails with selfishness or gossip or insecurity.

Also, of course, forgiveness. Learning how to forgive those who keep letting you down is hard, but your time here on earth is forgiveness school, and you'll get plenty of chances to learn this lesson.

You'll need God for that part. Ask Him for help forgiving and for giving second chances. Thank Him for forgiving you too.

Because this is your Lord—and He is so good at grace.

CONVERSATION SPARKS

1. Which friend is missing from this list? Tell about a friendship you have right now that can be difficult. What particular darkness does this friend bring into your life? Do you see yourself as any of these friends?

2. Read Colossians 3:12–14. What does this say about how we should love others? How has the Bible helped you to understand friendship?

3. What is your prayer for your friendships? What can God change in your heart to help you love yourself and others better?

SHINE ON!

Lord, You understand the kind of darkness that comes with hard friendships. You know what I need from my friends and how I can be a good friend. Please give me good friends who will help me follow You. I trust You to strengthen my faith so I can tell the world about You. In Jesus' name. Amen.

One Friday Morning in Santa Fe, Texas . . .

Back when I taught at a small Christian high school, there was a smart, responsible student named Jessica. I was the adviser for the school newspaper and yearbook, and she had a quiet faith that she shared once in a while in both of those.

Fast-forward more than a decade to 2018, when Jessica McNaspy was working as a chemistry teacher at Santa Fe (Texas) High School. She had graduated from Texas A&M with dreams of helping high school kids love chemistry as much as she does. (Or at least to help them pass the grisly subject.)

Jessica is married now and lives on the other side of Houston. I got to see her recently when my daughter, Catie, outgrew her pink-and-green bed and passed it down to Becca, Jessica's two-year-old.

Jessica loved teaching pre-AP chemistry in Santa Fe. The town of ten thousand is a close-knit community. Smack-dab between the hustle of Houston and tourism of Galveston, Santa Fe is a true gem of a Texas town. Families don't leave Santa Fe—many of Jessica's students' parents also went to the small high school.

Santa Fe was truly the last place where anyone expected tragedy to strike. People always say that about small towns, but Santa Fe was an especially sweet community. Crime was very low, neighbors looked out for one another, and churches were full on Sunday mornings. Even the name of the city means "holy faith" in Spanish. It could be called "quiet faith" to describe most of the citizens who worked hard, prayed hard, and wanted the best life for their families.

That's why when junior Dimitrios Pagourtzis burst into his high school with a shotgun and began shooting kids and teachers on May 18, 2018, it felt so horribly shocking. It would be weeks before police and witnesses could piece together what the killer did and why he did it. Even today, survivors struggle to talk about the tragedy without using words like *unbelievable*, *sickening*, and *horrific*.

During the twenty-five-minute shooting spree—the second deadliest in US history—Jessica was at the other end of the school with her pre-AP chemistry class. With only a few days until finals, Jessica had given her kids a free period. Many of her brainiac sophomores were exempt from taking their chemistry final, so Jessica offered them the rare chance to do whatever they wanted during her class. Because these were the pre-AP kids, lots of them used the free period to study for other finals. They spread out their books and papers and stretched out in the hall.

On the other side of the school, Dimitri, a former student of Jessica's, had walked through an open door by the art rooms. He wore a trench coat and held his father's gun. When he went into the art room and began shooting, a teacher pulled the fire alarm.

"As soon as I heard the fire alarm, I knew something was weird," Jessica said. "We had just had a fire drill the week before. And kids in other subjects were taking their AP tests. There's no way the school would interrupt the AP test for a fire drill."

As Jessica's chemistry kids gathered their phones and bags to evacuate for the fire alarm, she ran back into her classroom to turn off her red panel. This was the control box that ran the gas and electricity for her lab equipment. At that moment, she remembered that the other teachers on her team also had red panels in their classrooms. Those teachers were gone that day, though; both were in San Antonio for a basketball conference. Jessica knew that their subs, Mrs. Tisdale and Mrs. Perkins, were on the other side of the school.

What Jessica didn't know then was that those substitute teachers had to walk through the fine-arts hallway to evacuate for the fire alarm. They had to walk past the art room, where the mass shooting was playing out in real time. At the same moment that Jessica was wondering if she should go back to turn off their red panels, these teachers were trying to stop the shooter. They weren't able to. He killed them both instantly.

Back in the science wing, Jessica had no idea this tragedy was happening. Instead it felt like another Friday morning, another fire drill, another day before summer break would start. By the time she had evacuated her students, chaos had taken over the fine-arts wing on the other side of the school. Blood stained the halls, and students were slumped over. The nightmare was raging, and no one could stop it. Kids and teachers could only hide. Or run. Or pray.

Fire drill rules say that the students have to evacuate to the school's perimeter and wait through the drill in the grass—they can't stand on the sidewalk. But Jessica's kids didn't want to get their white shoes dirty from the mud. One of the sophomores tried to bribe his chemistry teacher. "Come on, Mrs. McNaspy. Please let me stay on the sidewalk," he teased. "I have Takis here. I'll share them with you if you let me on the sidewalk."

But by this time, Jessica was distracted by the commotion on the other side of the school. Students were helping injured kids escape through the double doors. Teachers sprinted onto the highway to stop the traffic that runs next to the high school. When the chem students noticed their English teacher standing in the middle of the highway in front of an eighteen-wheeler, screaming for it to stop, they realized something catastrophic was happening.

The head of the science department ran to Jessica. "Get the kids away from the school!" she yelled. "Get the kids across the highway NOW!"

Jessica didn't stop to think. She gathered her students to run across Highway 6 to Indian Automotive, a car shop. She was wearing Vans with no traction, but slipping while crossing the highway was the least of her worries. Something tragic was unfolding inside. The high school might be a giant explosive. Why else would they need to escape from it?

As the teachers hid the students behind the buildings at Indian Automotive, it was silent. What was happening? Everyone was terrified. No one could breathe.

Suddenly everyone's cell phones came alive with reports. Texts, emails, and Facebook messages from all over the world—all checking in to see if the news of a shooter was true. What was really happening there? What could they do?

Over and over Jessica told everyone contacting her the same story: "I'm fine. Pray that the kids will be fine."

There would be a lot of praying that day at Santa Fe High School. As the police took the shooter into custody, and as the students and teachers waited at the junior high for their parents to pick them up, the kids prayed with and for one another.

The staff gathered in a circle three different times to ask God to be with the students in the hospital, who were suffering from multiple gunshot wounds. They asked God to help the families who hadn't yet heard that their own kids were victims.

"We had never prayed together as a staff before. It's a public school," Jessica explained. "But this was all so different. We didn't know what else to do."

The rest of the day was as surreal as it was tragic. Jessica watched with her students as parents came to hug their kids and take them home. Then, as news trucks, more police, and comfort dogs came to the school, they watched as Santa Fe High School became the center of international news.

When she heard the reports that the shooter was Dimitri, her former student, she didn't believe it was true. He had been in her class the year before, and he had not been the kind of kid to start any trouble. Let alone this.

Jessica went home that night thanking God that He had protected her. Also, she found herself wondering what to say to her kids about what they had seen. Why did God let this happen? What would happen now?

Yellow crime-scene tape ringed the parking lot and grassy areas around Santa Fe High School. Law enforcement kept at a distance reporters, cameras, and anyone not shuttled in for official business. The building had become a war zone, a sacred place, a memorial.

For four hours on Saturday, school buses with police escorts shuttled students and staff from the junior high school to the high school to retrieve their belongings.

In the following days, Jessica would realize just how tragic the shooting had been. Her friends—the substitute science teachers— were heroes and victims. The teachers who had not been there that day carried guilt about it. She worried about the parents who had lost sons or daughters. And she worried about Dimitri's parents and the terrible guilt they would forever carry.

She wanted to know what to do.

GOD'S SILVER (GLITTER) LINING

There is nothing darker than the horror of a school shooting.

There are too many questions with no answers, too many images we keep replaying in our heads, too much loss, too much hate. It feels like there's no way we can find the light again. It feels like we should be very afraid. Life feels unsafe.

I have zero answers about school shootings. I don't know why God allows this to happen. I will never be part of a gun control debate because I feel like there are more questions than answers.

What I do know is that we live in a broken, hard world. Mass shootings, like what happened in Santa Fe, are sin raging at its worst. I do know this for sure: God always hates sin.

When God told His people in Isaiah 60:1 to "Arise, shine, for your light has come," He was giving real hope to an entire nation who had lived through horrific violence—like a school shooting— that kept happening over and over, every day, for generations. God's people had lost their way, and the Babylonians had taken over their country. Babylon was a vicious nation that punished the Israelites with bloodshed. They were not safe.

But the verses in Isaiah 60 that follow are filled with God's promises ("Arise, shine, for your light has come, and the glory of the LORD has risen upon you"). In John 14:27, He tells us, "Peace

I leave with you; My peace I give to you. Not as the world gives do I give to you. Let not your hearts be troubled, neither let them be afraid."

Read God's words of life, truth, and protection. Soak them in, over and over, praying them aloud, until they become so familiar.

Because even in our worst darkness, we don't have to be lost in fear. God is still on His throne and always loving us. Even in the worst moments of terror and sorrow, He never leaves us.

We cannot even imagine the expansiveness of God's love and protection. He doesn't leave us in our loneliness or our terror. He is constantly pulling us toward Him. He is always offering us the deeper spiritual blessings—forgiveness of our sins, peace, and a security that we belong to Him.

This is the message we want to share with the world. The light of Christ has come. Because of that, you can live confidently and securely in His love.

Forever.

CONVERSATION SPARKS

1. The phrase "fear not" is used eighty times in the Bible. Satan will try to use fear to pull us away from our Savior. Talk about this. How does fear and uncertainty distract you from Jesus? Share a specific story or example.

2. Read Isaiah 43:1. God actually commands us not to fear or worry. What prayer gives you comfort when you find yourself living in fear? How is shining for Jesus exactly the opposite of living in fear?

3. God saved you. Because of that, you can live confidently as His child. God is your rock, your hiding place, your hope. How can you trust in both His ability and in His desire to help you?

SHINE ON!

Heavenly Father, You love us and have perfect plans for us even when it seems that the world is hopeless. You've given us true hope through the light and love of Jesus Christ. Thank You for sending Your Son into our dark world. Thank You for taking care of us, even in the midst of the ugliest hate. Thank You for giving us everything good in our lives. In Jesus' name. Amen.

Timeline of a Crush

1. THE BIRTH OF YOUR CRUSH

The birth of every crush is sudden and fierce. Yours is no exception.

The boy, whom we will call Crush, has been your friend forever. But somehow, when he traded his glasses for contacts, it actually changed *your* vision—of him. What's going on here?

Suddenly, Crush is different from the boy who has always kicked your chair in English class and talked constantly about video games.

Is he taller? Definitely. But also, when did his shoulders get so broad? He seriously became Michael Phelps overnight. How do guys do this kind of magic? This kind of glow-up would have taken a female three years and hundreds of dollars at Sephora. But not Crush. He got a haircut, hit his growth spurt, and now he needs to be in a music video. Just. Wow.

Also, is he suddenly flirting with you? Because what is with all of these questions he keeps asking you about who you like and what you're doing this weekend and where you got your skirt? Guys don't really care about a fifteen-dollar skirt that you got on clearance at Old Navy. Do they?

Wait. Maybe Crush wants to buy a skirt like that for his mom—or his girlfriend? Does he have a girlfriend? Oh no. Maybe you're misreading his signals.

Nope. For sure, no girlfriend. And . . . WAIT. Has he always been flirting with you? Has he liked you for years? Was all this talk about video games and the constant teasing about your "nerdy" backpack really him trying to get you to notice him?

Now you have.

And you cannot stop thinking about him.

2. THE OBSESSIVE PHASE

What is this madness? Suddenly Crush is everywhere.

You see him at Target, when you're buying bras with your mom (a moment of silence for the creation of your official Most Embarrassing Moment). And now he has another reason to tease you.

Then, on Friday night, he's bowling RIGHT NEXT to your youth group, at the bowling alley where it's normally just old men. Coincidence? Surely not.

When you spot Crush skateboarding past your grandma's house, it becomes obvious that he must be thinking about you too because WHY ELSE WOULD YOU SEE EACH OTHER CONSTANTLY?

Or perhaps all your daydreaming about him is actually making him drop in on your everyday life? Are you really able to control this? Is God putting you together in all these weird moments for some predesigned plan of meeting? What else could explain Crush showing up at your lunch table to study science notes with your best friend?

These are the stories you will one day tell your grandkids. All the generations of your future family will gather on the porch swing, and Crush will report how he never really felt alive until that first English class with you.

He will probably get tears in his eyes as he recounts the details of never really knowing what he was born to do—until he spotted you and your new skirt walking into the room. That was the second when the world clicked into place so dramatically he could *feel* it.

3. THE SEASON OF DOUBT

This isn't actually going like you had hoped.

Because sometimes Crush is so mean to you. Like today when you dropped your phone in the hall. It was a bad drop, like facedown-on-the-linoleum bad. Crush was right there, and you had instant hopes that he would show you compassion and sympathy.

You expected him to put his hand on your shoulder and gently pick up your phone. He would slowly do the Fearful Flip for you to see if it was broken. Obviously, he would also hold your hand the whole time.

But instead he watched you do the Fearful Flip yourself. Then— just as you realized your screen was shattered—he laughed. And then he walked away!

This is not the kind of story anyone would ever tell grandkids. Because no matter what kind of phones are invented in the future, it will never be okay to walk away in the moment that someone else flips and finds a shattered screen.

Then the worst news comes, even worse than your mangled phone:

Crush has invited Smart Cheerleader to get iced coffee after school. WHAT IS THIS MADNESS? In first period, she's telling everyone how they spent the whole afternoon together, drinking iced coffee, eating scones, and studying.

Who drinks iced coffee? It is December. Why *iced* coffee? Is this some sort of secret signal to you that he doesn't really want to be with her? Maybe she's constantly texting him, and he finally took her out for a creepy date of iced coffee just to shake her off.

Because, BTW, scones? Really? For sure that's a fake date. No one eats *scones*. They're dry and weird, and this has GOT to be some desperate message to you that everything with Smart Cheerleader is so wrong.

But she is also very pretty and makes straight A's in AP classes without even studying. Because she seems to be spending a lot of time flirting with Crush in the hall. How much does she really need to touch her hair and giggle anyway? And isn't there some rule against the length of those cheerleading skirts? Because THAT IS NOT FINGERTIP LENGTH.

4. THE MOMENT OF TRUTH

Okay. You are a brave and strong girl, and Crush has consumed way too much of your brain space. It is officially time for the truth. No more waiting and wondering. At lunch, just as he walks into the cafeteria, you will pull him aside, and you will look him straight in the eye, and you will tell him exactly how you feel.

(Okay, of course, not exactly how you feel because bringing up your future college years together does seem a little crazy. Especially since he spends A LOT of time with Smart Cheerleader.)

This is it. He's walking into the cafeteria with about sixteen of his friends. (*Why, God? The prayer was for him to be alone.*)

But it's fine. You are strong and independent, and if movies have taught you anything, it's that ten seconds of courage can change everything. Except he is not really even looking at you. If he was expecting you to confess your love for him, wouldn't he at least notice you?

Stop overthinking! Just tell him how you feel. This is the moment when everything falls into place. This is where your life begins. No more quiet suffering about his brown eyes and wondering, "Did he like my Instagram post because he likes me, or does he really just like cute pictures of my dog?"

No turning back. This is the most important moment of your life.

(Except—really quick—a superfast prayer against cardiac arrest, because your heart is beating really fast and very loud. *Please, let my voice be stronger and louder than the thudding of my heart, Lord. Let me just get through this speech. Please.*)

"I've liked you for so long. I don't know if you feel the same way, but—"

Stop. Deep breath. In through the nose, out through the mouth. Don't pass out. Say it all. Right now. Ignore the surprise on his face. KEEP TALKING!

"You have been sending out mixed signals—" Pause. Deep breath. "I really think that you should be honest about your feelings for me—"

Wait. What? Why are his eyes so wide? Isn't this the moment when he gently takes your hand, leads you to a table, and begins to talk about your future together? Or at least maybe start nailing down prom details?

Keep going. Don't stop talking. Crush loves your boldness to get all your feelings out in the open. "I cannot stop thinking about you . . . I'm just kind of lovesick over you."

He is not leading you to a table. He is looking over his shoulder at his friends.

You have no choice but to grab his hand.

This turns out to be your fatal error.

He looks very afraid. Did he misunderstand and think you're *actually* sick? Grab harder. Hold tighter. "No! I'm not, like, flu sick. I'm sick over you—"

Noooo. He's REALLY pulling his hand away now. Why is he shaking his head? Oh no. No no no. Surely he just doesn't understand. There is some miscommunication going on. You should have texted all of this. No one talks face-to-face anymore. It's too risky.

Arghhhh! It's Smart Cheerleader. What is she doing here? Doesn't she have a calculus final to ace? Or a superspecial cheerleading meeting? Leave! Go and wear your tiny skirt around someone else. Crush and I are busy hashing out our relationship!

But you're not, actually, because he is grabbing HER hand and leading HER to a table. They are whispering, and she is consoling him. About what? About YOU? Oh, this is awful. All that adrenaline that made your heart race is now in the pit of your stomach, and you might really, actually, be sick all over the cafeteria.

Life is over. It's time for homeschool and never leaving your room.

5. THIS IS WHY THEY CALL IT A CRUSH

Everyone knows about your act of aggression toward Crush in the cafeteria.

Crush and Smart Cheerleader have spread the word about THE LAST MOMENT OF YOUR FORMER LIFE to everyone. They must be part of some sort of underground communication network because how in the world do the teachers know about this too? Even the freshman attendance secretary asked you if you're okay. The world definitely knows you are a very strange person who walks around talking about being sick about loving someone who doesn't even care about you.

Over the weekend, you cry so much that you are positive you have worn out your tear ducts. They will never be able to produce tears again. If something else tragic happens, you will be the stone-hearted freak who is dead to emotion.

Your true friends tell you that you'll be fine, but that is too hard to imagine right now. Because not only was there the tragic moment in the cafeteria where you (Cringe! Pain of embarrassment!) GRABBED HIS HAND, but you also still see him about a million times a day.

Now, you know the truth. By Valentine's Day, you'll be at some distant boarding school where there are only girls and hours of studying and where you'll train for your future life as an emotion-less hoarder who loves old newspapers more than actual people. Because, clearly, the only life you can handle is one where you are alone, with your cats, forever and ever.

6. LIFE MOVES ON. KIND OF.

Okay, you haven't had to quit school yet. Because, actually, some parts of this have turned out to be okay.

You even met a new friend; the quiet girl in Spanish class told you her crush story, which is a million times worse than yours. You couldn't even listen to the part about her making a SIGN FOR HIS LOCKER without covering your eyes. Because that's so much worse.

Now that Smart Cheerleader and Ex-Crush are the Darling Couple of the Entire School, you see that they deserve each other.

Seriously, how could you ever have believed that Ex-Crush was right for you? He and Smart Cheerleader are clearly meant for each other.

Proof? The number of selfies they take over iced coffee is a little crazy. A lot crazy. Does anyone else care that they are actually stunting their growth with all that caffeine?

Plus, you've learned the lesson that no boy is worth this kind of drama.

There must be something more worthy of your love . . .

GOD'S SILVER (GLITTER) LINING

Boys and relationships and crushes aren't the problem here. Ideally, one of these boys will end up becoming your partner—your husband—for life.

What is the problem, though, is the way that crushes and breakups and boyfriends can mess with your understanding of who you are. Because when you get *crushed* by a boy, or dumped by one, or really wrapped up in a lopsided relationship with one, it can send your self-worth some big messages.

Your feelings for and about boys can be so powerful that you kind of lose yourself. No one means for this to happen. But suddenly you might find yourself in a weird space where you are waiting for him to tell you if you're worthy or not. (Spoiler alert: you are.) This can feel like such a dark place because rejection and shame and pain from boys feel like the very biggest deal and very true.

Blame the hormones that make boys so irresistible right now. Or the fact that God designed this to be the exact stage when your body starts to get ready for what will lead to dates and real relationships and an engagement and a family and a house with a white-picket fence and sixteen grandkids.

Not yet, though. If all this relationship future is the ocean, you are just standing on the shore, letting the waves get your feet a little damp. You haven't learned yet how to swim in the big, crashing waves that come with love. Those lessons are learned slowly, and as you grow older.

First and most important, be sure you know who your life preserver is.

Jesus is your life preserver, your Savior, the one who gives you your true identity. He is the sure, steady flotation device that holds you as you learn to navigate the sharks and dangerous undertows of young love. He keeps your head above the rolling waves and your eyes focused on your future with Him.

Learn to hold on to your Savior as you venture into the world of first dates, painful crushes, and bad breakups. He will always (*always!*) hold you.

With the eternal and unsinkable love of your Savior, you can move through the waves, secure in the One who will never let you go.

CONVERSATION SPARKS

1. Tell your very worst crush story. What went wrong to cause the crush part of it? Specifically, why was it painful? What would you do differently next time?

2. What does God want for your relationships? In a few sentences, write (or share with the group) your thoughts about how God wants you to respond to crushes and dating.

3. Read Proverbs 3:5–6. Talk about what it means for you to trust God right now. What does this have to do with boys and relationships?

SHINE ON!

Dear Jesus, I need You to hold on to me through this next season. You are the one I can trust, the one who gives me faith and who will never leave me. Help me to believe that, deep in my soul, throughout all of my relationships. I love You, Lord. Amen.

Ten Signs You Might Be Addicted to Social Media

1. It's your major source of news.

For example, when you want to know if it's true that a celebrity died, your school is having a snow day, or what's going on with politics, you check Facebook first. CNN never even comes to mind.

2. Social media is your filter for the world.

Of course, you didn't watch the Super Bowl this year. You watched your Twitter feed ABOUT the Super Bowl. Okay, TBH, you watched your Twitter feed about the halftime show. (OKAY, FINE! Mostly about what everyone wore . . .)

3. It's literally always there.

You wake up by the sound of your dinging cell phone. You open it to check your DMs before you even wipe the sleep out of your eyes. Before your feet have touched the floor, you already know the status of your three closest friends. Before breakfast, you're all caught up on everyone's snaps, and by the time you're at school, you've watched all the new content from your favorite vloggers.

4. It's your friend finder.

Where is everyone? You could check in with them with a text or a phone call, but it is so much more convenient just to check Snapchat. Yes, it's weird and a little stalker-like, but this is not your fault. Your friends do not check their text messages, but they are very good at checking in at Starbucks, at the bowling alley, or the movies.

5. Life before social media sounds awful.

How did anyone plan a party, design a room, or pick out an outfit without Pinterest? This is what should be in history books—because how did your ancestors find out what professional organizers and wardrobe designers were recommending that day? How did they know what their friends liked? The concept of this feels as primitive as phones with cords and hunting buffalo for your dinner.

6. Your best teacher is YouTube.

How do you sew on a button? What's the right way to parallel park? make slime? slice up a watermelon? plunge a toilet? If the YouTube video with the most "likes" does not have the answer, then clearly it's impossible. Or not worth knowing.

7. The FBI needs your stalker abilities.

You can find anyone in the world through your followers and the followers of your closest 1,934 Instagram friends. Want to find the name of number 12 on the rival volleyball team or the boyfriend of the girl who lives next to your cousin or who your teacher was married to six years ago? Through the internet, you know absolutely everyone.

8. Your #goals are a little different.

Arguably the very greatest day of your life was the day when you captured an actual falling tree with your perfectly timed selfie. And it went legit viral. (Yes, it helped that you added the perfect caption: "If a tree falls in the woods and no one is there to selfie it, did it really fall?") To top off your historic moment of greatness, you got an LOL emoji from Lin Manuel Miranda's sister. You are absolutely adding this to all of your college applications.

9. You know the coward "unfriend" move.

You're not proud of it, but you have broken up with a friend, a boy-friend, or the Earth Club via social media. Yes, it's a little tacky—and totally impersonal—but sometimes the cleanest way to break ties is to just hit Unfriend.

10. You've become a bit spoiled.

Instagram figured out that you are really just there for the makeup tutorials and cute puppy stories. Now you always expect a tailored viewing experience. So, when you're watching actual, old-fashioned TV, it's weird to sit through whatever they show. Where is the Skip button for adult diaper commercials or sportscasters who talk about golf strokes?

GOD'S SILVER (GLITTER) LINING

Here is the real truth about social media: it's transforming our world, and the adults in your life have no idea where all of it is headed.

This new way to connect with one another is extremely powerful and always changing. Also, we're learning so much about ourselves. Social media makes us feel good when the world "likes" our pictures and videos.

But too much of it also makes us feel lonely.

No one is quite sure which parts of social media should be stopped and which should be promoted. It's a machine that needs to be controlled—but we don't know how to do that.

This is an interesting time to be a teenager because you'll probably be the generation that learns how to manage social media without letting it manage you. You will be the ones who teach us how social media doesn't have to be so isolating. You'll be the ones who put social media in its place. Because right now, it feels like we've all created little altars out of our profile pages. It feels like we're worshiping "likes" and "views" and "number of followers" with a passion that's unhealthy.

There are so many ways that we humans turn good things (connection with everyone in the world) into god things (those altars and our constant need for approval). In fact, the very first commandment God gives us is to not worship idols.

God gave us this commandment because He knows that humans love to make gods out of everything from cell phones to social media to "likes" to clicks. Idol worshiping is what happens when we find our worth in something we can hold in our hands, and social media is an absolute pit of this.

Ask God to help you here. Carve out time with your Savior in worship, in real rest, in reading the Bible, and in prayer. This is the true help that God gives you to keep you close to Him.

This is the true connection that your heart craves.

CONVERSATION SPARKS

1. Rate your relationship with social media right now. Be honest. ONE means that you don't even have it on your phone, and TEN means that this list feels like your real life.

2. Read 1 Timothy 6:6–10. Deep down, many of us believe one more thing will make us happy. Just one viral post or a hundred more followers or the well-orchestrated selfie that shows your life as perfect. Even if you've discovered this isn't true, even if you've found out the hard way that your insecurity itches deeper than social media approval can scratch, you probably keep trying. How do you see this in your own life?

3. When you find your identity in who others say you are, you devalue your identity as God's child. Pray for God to change your heart so you crave personal encounters with Christ through God's Word. What would it look like for church and Scripture to be the most sacred in your life?

SHINE ON!

Lord, You pull me back to You, even when I wander to find my value in what the world says is important. Help me to see that my forever identity is as Your daughter. Transform my heart so I want to live in that identity and do Your will. Thank You for Jesus, whose sacrifice means I'm Your forgiven child. In His redeeming name. Amen.

Savior Shines like Sequins

*And [Jesus] was transfigured before them, and
His clothes became radiant, intensely white,
as no one on earth could bleach them.*

—MARK 9:2–3

If you've ever smeared chocolate on your white jeans, you know the Five Stages of White Jeans Grief.

STAGE 1: DENIAL

It's not that bad—just a tiny blob of cupcake frosting. Rub it with a damp paper towel, and it'll disappear. No problem.

But wait. It's smearing more. Oh, and this is just fantastic. Now the three little drops of chocolate frosting are roughly the shape (and size) of Oklahoma, right on your upper thigh.

Wow. This definitely looks like poop.

STAGE 2: ANGER

You don't want to start drama—but this is totally your best friend's fault. It was *her* cupcake and *her* crazy story and *her* fault for gesturing

41

like an insane person and flinging frosting all over your pristine, beautiful, formerly white jeans.

(Plus, she has always been a klutz. Is there some kind of an intervention for people who cannot control their bodies and are constantly flinging frosting?)

STAGE 3: BARGAINING

Bleach. That's the magic potion to pour on this. You'll just run down to the chemistry lab and ask for a big bottle of Clorox.

If your teacher thinks that's weird, explain you're doing a little bonus lab about the effect of whatever-the-chemical-symbol-for-chlorine-is on your (formerly) perfect white pants. They'll be as good as new, and you will forever stay away from any frosting flingers (side-eye to you, best friend telling a story).

STAGE 4: DEPRESSION

Okay, now your life is as ruined as your pants. It's not your fault that your chemistry teacher's reaction was *a little over the top*. She was so excited about showing the chemical reaction of bleach—until it totally didn't work. The Chocolate Oklahoma would not be erased, even with straight Clorox.

For the next twenty minutes, she talked all about the resistance in the fabric of your white pants. She offered to show you a true chemical reaction in a petri dish. Which . . . what? Who cares about chemical reactions?

Now you've missed the rest of lunch, and you still look like you had an accident in your white pants.

STAGE 5: ACCEPTANCE

Clearly there are two types of girls in the world: those who can wear white jeans—and you. This ruins so many outfits for you. You'll probably have to wear a floral print for your wedding because white is now dead to you.

This is your lot in life. At least you have an eyes-wide-open understanding of what a letdown cleaning supplies really are.

~~~~~~~~~~

Just kidding about the white jeans grief—kind of.

Because it is true that even bleach is powerless against the toughest stains. But talking about bleach brings us to Mark's picture of Jesus at His transfiguration. When Mark reaches for the very best description of what holy, sacred, brilliant, glowing Jesus looks like, he tries for the comparison of some freshly bleached white linen.

But—nah—that doesn't do it. Jesus is even more brilliant than that. Another disciple, Matthew, tries to draw a picture of Jesus in this amazing moment as "His clothes became white as light" (Matthew 17:2).

It's the disciple Luke who has the best word to describe Jesus after His transfiguration—he calls the Savior "dazzling" (Luke 9:29).

The transfiguration was the moment when Peter, James, and John (Jesus' disciples) understood who their Friend really was. You can hear their awe in Peter's suggestion that they should all stay right here forever, on this mountain—in this moment—forever.

Over the next few pages, let's look at what this transfiguration meant for Jesus' best friends and His disciples. There was no doubt about it now—they really were hanging out with the Savior of the world, the Messiah they'd heard about all their lives. This was life changing. Once they realized they had access to the promised

Redeemer, the Christ, God's own Son, they couldn't un-know that. (For us too, but we'll get into that.)

Once the disciples understood Jesus' true identity, they knew the full story. God had done what He promised and sent the Messiah. Anything was possible; most important, heaven was now a definite promise. Also—and this is important—the same power that transfigured Jesus was also in them. They could live as new creations.

You and I are new creations too. That's what Baptism does. The dazzling, brighter-than-bleach light of our Savior is inside each and every one of us. The Holy Spirit is always molding us to become more like our Savior, for our souls to become brighter than light.

In this section, we'll look at how it can be hard to leave the old parts of your sinful past behind. Also, it can be so exhilarating when you're experiencing your own spiritual glow-up, right in the middle of your mundane life, that it might be hard to go back to ordinary life. Finally, when God offers to transform you to be more like Him, you will realize that this is what you wanted all along.

For now, let's just take one more moment to thank God for giving us a Savior like Jesus—who shines as brightly as sequins.

If You Give a Girl a Mountain(top) Experience

(A Silly Parody with an Everlasting Meaning)

If you give a girl from the plains of Nebraska a job at a summer camp on an actual mountain in Colorado, she will probably be very nervous when she arrives.

At the staff introductions, when you ask her to share her favorite Bible verse, she will probably say "John 3:16" because it is the only one her petrified brain can remember at that moment. She will feel like a complete spiritual loser and worry she will be ejected from the Christian camp for "knowing absolutely zero about the Bible."

The girl will want to fit in so badly. She will worry constantly about her hair (suddenly flat in this dry heat) and her clothes (which lack the trendiness of Colorado and the certain Birkenstock-cool of camp). The girl will feel fat and promise herself she won't eat any of the homemade chocolate chip cookies—and then she will accidentally eat seven.

When you move the girl far from home, she will write letters to her friends back in Nebraska. She will complain that no one likes her and that she is so out of place. She will replay the terrible Bible verse moment seven million times and want to go back in history and shut her own mouth every single time.

But if you put the girl right smack-dab in the middle of a Christian camp, she will realize that this whole new world is so much more than just memorizing Bible verses. She will start to relax. Together with the other counselors, she will work hard to prepare the mountainside camp for the kids who are coming. They'll plan a whole summer of s'mores and Capture the Flag and ways to teach the kids about the true Jesus. Slowly—and then all at once—this girl will realize that she is exactly where she needs to be.

After just a couple of nights around the campfire, the girl will completely fall in love with these new worship songs, the stories of transformation the camp leaders share, and the billions of twinkling stars in God's creation. She will sense something shifting and tingling in her soul. She'll realize this is God working through all those worships. It's the Holy Spirit speaking to her through the Bible verses she memorizes. When she hears other teenagers say they love God, she will be so encouraged that she will say this same thing herself—over and over and with conviction.

Instead of watching Transformation Makeup Tutorials, she will live out her own *actual* transformation. She will watch as her new friends share their testimonies about how they were the hundredth sheep that Jesus went back for, how they were the prodigal son, how they were completely lost from their Lord—but He still loved them. While listening to all of this, the girl will better understand who she is and what she is worth to God.

Emojis and "likes" on Instagram have never felt so far away.

If you give the girl the mountaintop experience, the friends to worship with, and the 24/7 of Jesus, she will begin to see herself as her Savior sees her. She will not need to check her hair or hate her thighs or trash anyone who gets on her nerves.

Every day she will wake up praising God and excited about the very beautiful soul He has restored in her. She will read the Bible to see who she is—instead of reading the blogs that insist on Top Ten Changes to Make You Beautiful.

Eventually, this girl will wonder who she will become if she ever has to leave this place. She wants only to be at camp with these people and these campfire worships and all this time with Jesus forever. Coming down from this mountain sounds impossible.

Maybe she will never go home. She'll concoct a plan to live in a tent, right next to the kitchen (with those delicious cookies) forever and ever. Because what is the alternative? Leave camp in two weeks when it's over? Go back to spending two hours *trying to take the perfect bathroom selfie?* Never! She doesn't want to go back to that shallow, dull life. The thought of it makes her march straight to the camp director and announce that she is sending for her things to stay forever.

If you give a girl a mountaintop, a spiritual transformation, and she wants to live inside that transformation forever, you will need to talk to her about Peter, and how he wanted to live forever on a mountaintop with his best friends and his Savior. You will need to remind the girl that Jesus told Peter not to be afraid and then led him down from the mountain.

After you tell the girl about Peter, explain to her that the rest of the world also needs the message she's learned at camp. Remind her that her soul (where the transformation has happened) is inside her body. This is very good news because she can take her soul back to Nebraska with her. You'll probably need to remind her that the Holy Spirit is a living, breathing part of her in every single way. She literally cannot escape that—which is the best promise in the world.

If you give a girl a mountain, where she has the true mountaintop experience of a spiritual transformation, you will tell her to pray for God to seal all of His wisdom and value in her soul. You will remind the girl that she knows now how to reflect God's love to the world. She knows what it means to *shine*.

Finally, when this girl leaves the mountain—when she goes back to the world and the pressure to be perfect, to the hard relationships, to the terrible insecurity—she really is going to be okay. She now understands everything the praise songs proclaim. She has felt what the psalmist meant when he wrote that the Lord gives us everything and there is nothing else we could want. This girl knows that she will never again sit unimpressed at an Easter service.

Because she has experienced the same power that raised Jesus from the dead.

GOD'S SILVER (GLITTER) LINING

If you've experienced a mountaintop high like this, you know how it feels to want to bottle up the moment forever. After feeling this kind of brilliant faith and trust in your Savior, are you really supposed to go back to just normal life—wading through silly insecurity and listening to endless gossip?

The answer is yes.

And no.

You will never go back to who you used to be because you have been changed forever. Once you realize that God truly loves you completely and forever, you *know* that, in a soul-deep way.

The answer is also that, yes, you do have to go back to real life. (Remember, though, you are changed now.)

God promises that whatever may come, you will always be His precious daughter, for every breath, for every moment, and for all the moments that take your breath away. In every situation, regardless of how good or how bad, God is always there, forever giving you His power, always loving you. You can trust this (Psalm 71:5).

You can trust you know who you are—because of who He is and what He does in your life.

Hold on to that power and promise.

For eternity.

CONVERSATION SPARKS

1. Tell about a time (summer camp, a retreat, a worship service) when you experienced a spiritual mountaintop high. Describe how this felt during and afterward.

2. Talk about Peter's reaction to Jesus' transfiguration in Mark 9:5. Can you blame Peter for his shock? How do you think you would have reacted to witnessing Jesus transforming before you?

3. Read Matthew 17:5–8. How do the disciples react to God's holiness and announcement? Why do they react like this? How does Jesus respond to the disciples' fear?

SHINE ON!

Dear Jesus, You are so loving, so gracious, so faithful. Thank You for the moments of incredible transformation. Thank You also for being with me in all the other moments. Remind me of Your faithfulness when I struggle to believe. Fill me up with Your light. Help me shine it to the rest of the world, all the time. In Your name. Amen.

What Do You Want . . . More?

Jesus' Question Can Transform Your Faith

My Uncle Fred wasn't really my uncle. He and his wife, Aunt Katie, were my parents' best friends. My parents had introduced Uncle Fred and Aunt Katie to each other, and when I had kids of our own, Aunt Katie and Uncle Fred showed up and helped us raise our kids. They were the kind of family friends who become more family than friend.

For all of these reasons, we were devastated when our beloved Uncle Fred was diagnosed with inoperable brain cancer three years ago. And so sad when God took him to heaven last January.

Uncle Fred showed us so much about battling with a deadly disease without losing faith. When our family visited him in the hospital, Uncle Fred taught our kids, "Kneel next to my bed so I can see you when you pray with me."

Later, when Uncle Fred was very sick and we didn't know what to pray, he taught us to sing. One of us would repeat "Alleluia" over and over until someone would offer a verse ("You are Lord, Jesus. Alleluia. Alleluia. Alleluia.").

Actually, Uncle Fred had always been our teacher. He showed us, through his ministry of questions and prayers, how to share Jesus with strangers. Every day for years, Fred asked waitresses, garbage men, and kids in his Sunday School class this question:

What do you want Jesus to do for you today?

Guess what? Everyone—doctors and nurses and grocery store clerks—had an answer to this question. No one ever said, "Why do I care about Jesus?" or "That's a personal question" or "None of your business." Ever.

They answered Fred's question like it was a divine invitation from the Holy Spirit. They told him their most personal stories.

These strangers looked Fred in the eye and talked to him about soul matters they were thinking about—but no one else had asked them about. Then he prayed with each person, right there. Over and over I saw the importance of this question.

A typical exchange might go like this:

~~~~~~~~~~~~~

Sarah the Waitress [*approaching the table*]: "Hi! My name is Sarah. I'll be taking care of you today."

Uncle Fred: Hi, Sarah, I'm Fred. I'm so happy to meet you. Can I ask you a question?

Sarah the Waitress [*smile frozen on her face*]: Umm . . . sure.

Uncle Fred: What would you like Jesus to do for you today?

Sarah [*expression changes from professional to vulnerable*]: I want Him to help my son, John, get a job. He has three interviews this morning, and he really needs this chance at something better.

Uncle Fred: Lord, be with John today. Please help him to find work. Lead him in the interviews to find the job that's right for him. Help him to be secure in You, dear God. Please give Sarah peace as she is working here today, and always, Lord. Thank You that she's here to help all of us have a good lunch. In Jesus' name. Amen.

Sarah [*as she wipes away tears*]: Thank you. Thanks so much.

~~~~~~~~~~~~~

Do you see what happened here? Uncle Fred prayed for what Sarah asked. He also prayed for her son to know Jesus and for her to know peace. Yes, Sarah wants her son, John, to find work, but God will also give her what she wants more.

How did Fred know this was what Sarah wanted? Because these are the things we all want. Deeper security, soul repair, trust that God is taking care of us.

Listen to Jesus' conversations with people He met, and you'll find that He often went deeper into their desires—until He got to what they wanted *more*.

When Jesus talked to the blind man in Luke 18:41, He asked him, "What do you want Me to do for you?"

The blind man said, "Lord, let me recover my sight."

Jesus did heal the man (v. 43), but He also gave the man what he wanted more. Jesus gave him the security of a relationship with his Savior; He gave him faith that the other people in the crowd didn't seem to have. They had told the blind beggar to leave Jesus alone, but the man "cried out all the more" (v. 39).

At the end of the story, Jesus gave the man a future. The blind man is now praising God and walking with Jesus. This was what he wanted *more*.

This is what we all want more. We want eternal security. We want mercy. We want to be fully known and fully loved. We want to experience the kind of joy that comes from a life of walking alongside our Savior and praising our Lord.

GOD'S SILVER (GLITTER) LINING

What do you want right now?

Something shallow might come to mind first (red velvet cake pops, to lose five pounds, for that boy to like you, that friend to be sorry she hurt you, a little more spending money, popularity, more friends, a fun vacation, cute clothes, better hair, revenge . . . you get the idea).

But then ask yourself the harder, deeper question: What do you want *more*?

Here's where you'll find your soul-level desires, the ones that are gnawing at your spirit in the way that really matters.

As Jesus taught the woman at the well, there are surface desires—like something to eat or drink. But then there are the deeper remedies, the ones that will truly quench your soul. These are total forgiveness of your sins, eternal life with your Savior, peace, acceptance, and knowing that you are loved.

Jesus told the Samaritan woman at the well, "Everyone who drinks of this water will be thirsty again, but whoever drinks of the water that I will give him will never be thirsty again. The water that I will give him will become in him a spring of water welling up to eternal life" (John 4:13–14).

Everything else we want will keep us thirsty for more. Lots of friends? Fun—but not what you need more. A hundred dollars in your new cute purse? Good—but not what you need more. A dozen glazed doughnuts? Delicious—but not what you need more. A viral social media post? Delightful—but not what you need more.

What you need more is a transformation of your soul. This is what Jesus gave the blind man, what He told the Samaritan woman about, and what the disciples saw up on the mountain at His transfiguration. This is what Uncle Fred was getting to when he prayed with all those thirsty people.

When God changes our souls, He changes our lives. This is what we want more—deeper security that transforms every part of our lives.

CONVERSATION SPARKS

1. What do you want Jesus to do for you right now?

2. How does the answer to the question "What do you want more?" relate to spiritual transformation in your personal life?

3. Read Luke 18:39 and talk about the blind man's faith. What does it tell you about him that he "cried out all the more"? What did he trust about Jesus? Do you have this same trust? What can you pray about your faith?

SHINE ON!

Lord, You understand what I want more. Thank You for changing me for eternity. Help me to share this message with the world, who needs to know Your love. Please keep growing my faith in You, Lord. In Jesus' name. Amen.

Ten Steps to Transform Your Bedroom

(One Step to Transform Your Soul)

1. Decide you hate EVERYTHING about your current bedroom.

Just sitting in this stifling space is punishment. The reasons are almost too numerous to name, but here are a few: the *horrible* paint color (Pretty Princess Pink), the furnishings (many bad experiments with chalkboard paint), and a bookshelf that is overcrowded with every ribbon, trophy, and certificate ever awarded to you.

Actually, as you discover when you inspect one towering stack of certificates, some of these belong to your brother. He dumped them in here when all this clutter threatened to take over his room.

As you begin to tear apart your disgusting room, you discover a total of eight journals. Most of them are completely blank after the first page because you are a person who promises to "write every single day!" and then immediately stops.

This is pathetic. No wonder you've been in a bad mood the past month—you are surrounded by chaos, failed projects, and your brother's achievements.

2. Transformation begins with inspiration.

Pinterest inspires you (obviously). So do catalogs, your friends' bedrooms, the aisles of Hobby Lobby, the color of the cheery red wagon outside, and your little sister's chocolate milk mustache. Ideas are literally everywhere you look.

You are so ready to turn your tiny corner of the world into a cozy, modern, trendy, organized nest that features fairy lights and a cool bed that hangs from your ceiling. This new room will be an explosion of color. It will be a study in funky beauty.

In this dream version of your room, it's also expanded to the size of Hogwarts—also, it's more ornate. Your fantasy room will smell like a mixture of peppermint essential oil and a field of daisies (even though you have a bad habit of leaving wet towels on your floor).

In this fever of fantasy, you also keep your room completely organized all the time. To be honest, even in your inspired state, this feels a little far-fetched. But, whatever.

Nothing—not even reality—can dull the image you have of your perfect bedroom.

3. Purge, purge, purge.

In the span of one afternoon, pull everything out of your room. Throw away crumbling science projects from your STEM era. (Really? A Styrofoam model of the solar system? Why have you saved this for so many years?) Toss out a stash of Halloween candy you forgot about for, oh, maybe a decade?

You are ruthless. You are getting rid of all the things, even the Barbie collection that was the biggest in the whole second grade and your favorite Trolls nightgown that you wore every single night for two years.

It's all out of here. Books? Give them away! Weird clothes (looking at you, overalls and bright pink rain boots) must be donated! Every note your best friend passed to you in elementary school? You don't need them. This junk is standing between you and a gorgeous new space.

4. Get ALL THE THINGS!

In a spending frenzy, you buy paint, brushes, weird rugs, funky curtains, silly signs about unicorns, and real-life butterflies, mounted under glass. Everything has possibility. Sure, the beanbag chair is a strange mustard yellow, it makes you sweat, and it smells like burnt tires. But it's on clearance! Get it!

Spend hours on Instagram finding inspiration in all kinds of hashtags: #rustichippie, #fleamarkettrendy, #cushcountry, #bougiebutcheap, and #ironic.

Watch way too many design shows, each with the same message: When You Change Your Space, You Change Your Life.

Become so inspired that you convince your mom to drive you to the actual city dump. As she helps you load up a dozen used candles, she mentions "more clutter" under her breath.

But you know better! You are a fun, whimsical designer who creates unusual spaces with reclaimed pieces. You are practically your own HGTV show. Your taste is unique, and your dedication to your dream bedroom is endless. Funky old bottles, a moth-eaten tarp, and a cracked disco ball—this will all look unbelievable.

5. Fatigue sets in.

You are suddenly very tired. It's all too much, with the complicated color scheme and all the stuff that needs to be repaired or sewn or painted or just cleaned.

Also, you've lost the vision for what the elephant wallpaper was really going to do for that corner. How, exactly, does it go with the cowhide rug? Was your plan here to be ironic? Or have you really just collected all of this crazy stuff that looks like—well—*garbage*?

Pile the weird things in the corner of your room for a solid month, waiting for the energy to actually start the transformation.

Go back to your boards on Pinterest to reclaim a little of your original enthusiasm. But suddenly, you notice the designer rooms have a total of three pieces of furniture, and most of them are bright white. One red rug. A single piece of statement art. These rooms have one accent wall—not an entire accent room of camo wall hangings like you planned.

Realize that your style is actually Plain Minimalist.

And your room is now Hoarders.

6. Just do it!

Okay, this has become ridiculous.

Give yourself a stern lecture about constantly overthinking everything. Admit that you are actually afraid that you have no talent for room decoration and that you will ruin everything.

Ask God (Creator of literally everything) to give you the energy and inspiration to change just a little corner of your room today. He created the oceans in one day—surely He can help you set up a little reading nook.

The next day, feel a bit better. Repeat, "It's just paint . . . it's just paint," and slap some white paint on your ugly pink wall.

7. Progress. Finally.

The white paint helped a lot.

Maybe you really only needed to update your walls from those years when you thought cotton candy was the most beautiful color.

As it turns out, white really is the perfect paint color. Even the oversized periodic table in the bright orange frame doesn't look *too* odd on this new wall.

With the white walls, you see that you don't need most of this other stuff to transform your room. You really should return the black mosquito netting that you planned to hang around your bed.

(Because, huh? How is wrapping black nets around your bed *ever* a good idea?)

Onward with the white paint. You're getting somewhere (*finally!*).

8. Purge. Again.

Hold a small garage sale of your own to get rid of some of the weirder "treasures" you bought in your naïve youth (last month). Admit to yourself you will never have the time to sand, stain, and fix the old coffee table you found in your grandma's basement.

When your neighbor gets really excited about a bright green rug you got at Goodwill, feel generous, hand it to her, and say, "May your room surpass your greatest Pinterest dreams."

And you mean it. Even though your future projects will be smaller in scale.

9. Time to show off.

Invite your two best friends over for a Reveal Party, just like your favorite design show does.

When they ooohh over your newly purged closet and ahhhh over the gold-glitter accent wall you created by gluing actual glitter on old frames, hug them (and accidently cover them with glitter). Because, yes! This does look good!

Give them advice like "You can't be afraid of change!" and "Accept that nothing will look exactly like you expect."

Finally, tell them, "God gave us bright blue oceans and fields of peonies and trees in every color. Don't you think He is a creator who takes beauty seriously? Shouldn't we do the same?"

They are amazed by your wisdom, and as you post all of this on Instagram, you use your new signature hashtag, #createliketheCreator. Realize you might have exactly the right vision/courage/energy to become the next famous teen designer. You could do this.

It will all start with your own YouTube channel called "Teen Transformations!" complete with inspirational quotes plucked straight from your own wisdom and experiences.

This is probably your calling in life. You will have a thriving business before you graduate from high school. You'll be a household name, synonymous with the transformation of teen bedrooms all over the world.

("Let's begin with white paint" will be your signature wisdom.)

10. Reality. Again.

Have an awkward conversation with your dad about what you're going to do with the half-empty paint cans in the garage. Also, the human-size chess pieces you had (wrongly) thought would look fun in your room.

Try to explain that you are just starting your career as a person who helps transform bedrooms for those poor souls who don't have your talent.

When he brings up the money you owe him for your new curtains, drop the subject completely.

Accept that (for now) your design talent might be limited to just your own room. (Although you do still watch design shows, secretly convinced that you could "do it better.")

GOD'S SILVER (GLITTER) LINING

So, yes, room makeovers can be hard to pull off. In your head, there are just a couple of steps between Before and After.

Reality looks a lot like the process above. Many bad ideas, more steps backward than forward, and terrible regrets about furniture buys. Trying the transformation process can be so daunting, you might just decide to stick with the same old, same old room.

There's another kind of transformation, which Paul describes in Ephesians 2. This one is different from what happens with your room redo though. Paul tells us the dramatic way we change from "dead" in sin (Ephesians 2:1) to "immeasurable riches of His grace" (v. 7).

Let's look more closely at the makeover Paul describes. He starts with a detailed description of our "before" picture. *We are dead in sin . . . we always go along with the world's bad ideas . . . most of us are following Satan around . . . no hope for any of us* (see Ephesians 2:1–3).

Then Paul gets to his point: the Good News, the transformation. In verses 4–6, he tells us, "But God, being rich in mercy, because of the great love with which He loved us, even when we were dead in our trespasses, made us alive together with Christ—by grace you have been saved—and raised us up with Him and seated us with Him in the heavenly places in Christ Jesus."

This really is an instant, one-step makeover. God really did change everything when He sent Jesus to die for our sins. Because our Father loves us so much, we don't have to stay in our "before" picture of our sin.

When Jesus was transfigured up on the mountain, it was another moment of instant transformation. A bright cloud, God's voice, and an incredible moment of realization for the disciples—all in one split second.

This was divine transformation. Instant and miraculous.

When you try to transform your own spiritual life, the process can feel like the tediousness of trying to transform your bedroom. You try to become a better person on your own, but you keep botching it.

This is why Paul's wonderful words in verses 8–10 feel so hopeful. "For by grace you have been saved through faith. And this is not your own doing; it is the gift of God, not a result of works, so that no one may boast. For we are His workmanship, created in Christ Jesus for good works, which God prepared beforehand, that we should walk in them."

This is the difference between any human makeover and what God does for you. It's not your effort or your talent or your goodness that makes the transformation from sinner to saved. Paul is clear about this. You were dead in your sin, and God made you alive in Christ.

CONVERSATION SPARKS

1. Have you ever attempted a room redo? Tell about your experience. What worked and what didn't? What part of the transformation was the most challenging?

2. Read Ephesians 2. Talk about the spiritual makeover that happens to each of us. Who does Paul say does the work (miracle) here? Why does he point out that it's God and not us?

3. Read Ephesians 6, Paul's instructions for spiritual war-
    fare. Paul includes these instructions for staying strong
    in your faith a few chapters after his description of our
    spiritual transformation. Why do you think he includes
    this encouragement for believers?

SHINE ON!

Dear Lord, thank You so much for transforming me from my sin.
You loved me when I was totally dead and couldn't do anything to
help myself. Your love changed everything. Help me to trust You.
Give me faith to live in the transforming grace of Your perfect love.
In Jesus' name. Amen.

Add Glitter to Your Soul

(God Can Transform You through Meditation on His Word)

What You Need

1 Bible verse (there are lots, so find your favorite)
1 child of God (you)
60 breaths (we'll get to that)
1 Holy Spirit (always with you)
10 minutes (every day)

The Problem

Are you worn out by so many hours of comparing yourself with others? Do you often feel like you're left out? Do you believe that everyone else is loved, but people secretly don't like you?

Are you ready to know true love? Do you want to finally feel secure? Are you interested in sharing this sparkling, beautiful love with the people in your life?

HERE'S HELP!

1. There are 31,102 verses in the Bible. Choose your favorite.

It's time to find your favorite Bible verse.

Choose one that tells you who you are, who God is, and how much He loves you. Here are some you might like:

> ✳ 1 Peter 2:9 is about being chosen. ("But you are a chosen race, a royal priesthood, a holy nation, a people for His own possession, that you may proclaim the excellencies of Him who called you out of darkness into His marvelous light.")

- Zephaniah 3:17 tells about God's fantastic love for you. ("The LORD your God is in your midst, a mighty one who will save; He will rejoice over you with gladness; He will quiet you by His love; He will exult over you with loud singing.")

- Romans 8:28 reminds you that God is in control, no matter what. ("And we know that for those who love God all things work together for good, for those who are called according to His purpose.")

- Isaiah 41:10 helps you know God's power over fear. ("Fear not, for I am with you; be not dismayed, for I am your God; I will strengthen you, I will help you, I will uphold you with My righteous right hand.")

To help you choose a verse, talk to other people about which ones they love. Ask your parents, your youth leader, your friends. Think back to your confirmation verse.

You can also Google verses (of course) to search for verses about specific topics, or read your favorite Bible story to see if any particular phrasing really speaks to you. The Bible is full of powerful messages with the exact perfect wording. Go get yours.

After you've chosen your verse, memorize it well. Say it over and over until you've learned it, deep in your heart. When you wake up in the morning and you're stumbling to the bathroom, glance in the mirror at the mascara under your eyes and the rat's nest of your hair and say your verse. (Maybe it's "You are altogether beautiful, my love; there is no flaw in you," Song of Solomon 4:7.)

You could also use James 1:17. When you're in the shower and the water is massaging your back and you're combing conditioner through your hair, say your verse to yourself. ("Every good gift and every perfect gift is from above, coming down from the Father of lights, with whom there is no variation or shadow due to change.")

As you wash your face at night, remember your Baptism, and say the words of 1 Peter 3:21 to yourself. ("Baptism, which corresponds to this, now saves you, not as a removal of dirt from the body but as an appeal to God for a good conscience, through the resurrection of Jesus Christ.")

Throughout your day, find times to say the words of your verse. As you walk into your impossible geometry class, remember John 16:33. ("I have said these things to you, that in Me you may have peace. In the world you will have tribulation. But take heart; I have overcome the world.")

As you step into the cafeteria, where your best friend isn't speaking to you because she's in a snit about your homecoming plans, take a deep breath and chant your verse to yourself. (Maybe it's 1 Peter 4:8, which says, "Above all, keep loving one another earnestly, since love covers a multitude of sins.")

Your personal Bible verse can be your refrain throughout your day. Say it like a desperate prayer when you are feeling drained and unlovable. Say it like a praise song when the sunshine breaks through the clouds in your soul and the warmth of your Savior's love spreads inside you.

2. Make the most important appointment of your life. Show up every day.

Make a specific appointment with God's Word that you won't miss. Set an alarm on your cell phone to remind yourself to spend time in the Bible every day.

What time works best for you? Maybe you're a morning person (then try waking up ten minutes earlier). Perhaps you're a night person (then try going to bed ten minutes later). Maybe choose ten minutes right after school or practice. Rather than wasting an hour on YouTube, you can do this spiritual practice.

Establishing a routine will help make meditating on God's Word a habit for you. Show up at this prescribed time and God will already be waiting there for you.

3. Now is the time for glittering—deep in your soul.

Let's call this next step "glitter getting" because that's one way to describe what God is doing in your soul. Your heavenly Father gave you His Word to encourage and inspire you. It's powerful. Here's how He puts the brilliance (glitter) of His strong words into your mind, your heart, and your soul.

First, set a timer for ten minutes. Find a comfortable and quiet place to lie down. Close your eyes. Place your hands on your belly and feel your breath in and out. In and out.

(Yes, this is boring, but it's important.)

Try to clear all the other thoughts from your head. No matter what distractions are around you, focus on the way your stomach rises with breaths in and deflates with breaths out.

No fair thinking about if your stomach is too fat or too thin. Ignore the dinging of text messages on your phone. Tune out the conversation in the other room about the football team. Forget that you were going to play video games with your brother right now. Your single job in this moment is to feel your breath.

God designed your breath to be the engine of your whole body. When you pay closer attention to the constant miracle of breath, it calms your mind. (Also, you'll use your breath later on to remind you of important truths.)

While you're lying in your quiet place, take a quick scan of your body. Feel the sensations of heaviness in your arms and legs. Let your body tell you about any tensions it's feeling right now. Let your mind recognize these—then focus again on your breath.

As you breathe in and out, recite your Bible verse to yourself over and over. If you start to become distracted—about how you should really feed your cat right now and that's why he's meowing in your ear, or about how much math homework you have, or how you really hope that your cute neighbor is behind the lawn mower you hear starting next door—focus again on how your breath feels going in and out.

For ten minutes (until you hear the timer ding) say your Bible verse to yourself over and over. If you want, you can also add another thought that reminds you of your identity: "God loves me so much." Or "God chose me." Or "Jesus died for me." Or "The same power that raised Jesus from the dead is in my soul right now." Or "The Holy Spirit lives inside me forever and ever."

Take one more ginormous, slow breath in and out. Say a prayer for the Holy Spirit to seal this message in your soul.

This is meditating on God's Word. Your Father can use this time-out from your busy life to settle the truth of His love deep into your soul.

4. Sow the glitter and grace to everyone you know.

Now is the fun part. You will get to experience an actual miracle. The Word of God is inside of you. This is the glitter. Faith is sparking through your soul. God put it there when you were baptized, and it's yours to share with the world.

Go into your day carrying the love of your Savior. This is your supernatural power, and it's yours to call on whenever you need it. This is your strength to latch onto when you are weak. Most of all, this love is your answer when you question what you're worth.

As soon as the enemy whispers that you are not loved, tune in to your breathing. As you breathe in, remember your Bible verse and recite it to yourself. Feel the creation that God has done perfectly in you. Remember right then who you are. Remember God's love for you and that He chose you to be His daughter. He is holding you.

Then, when the friend drama starts up, you don't have to be part of it. You have a different layer to yourself. Ask God to use your breath to remind you. He will connect you to the deeper, richer, more nutritious stuff inside you than the fights with the girls who are running on fumes right now.

They need the glitter you have pulsing through your soul. They need the message you have. You can share it with them.

GOD'S SILVER (GLITTER) LINING

Guess what? You can shine this message to the world. God's Word shows you that you have this security all the time. The Holy Spirit will remind you of it every time you hear Jesus' Gospel preached in church and every time you remember your Baptism. Your deep breathing will tune your mind into the message. This is the Holy Spirit spreading the glitter of faith through your soul and into your life.

Meditation is one way to connect your mind to the power of the Holy Spirit in your personal Bible verse. A reminder from your Savior, about His great love for you, can change your thoughts, your spirit, and your life.

This is transformation through meditation on the sweet love of your Savior.

Share it with the world, dear girl.

This is what it means to shine.

This is what it means to reflect God's love.

CONVERSATION SPARKS

1. What Bible verse did you choose? Why this one? Tell the specific message about God this verse teaches you.

2. Read Hebrews 4:12; Romans 10:17; and 2 Timothy 3:16. What do these verses say to you?

3. Psalm 119:11 proclaims, "I have stored up Your word in my heart, that I might not sin against You." Here, the psalmist describes the spiritual practice of meditating on God's Word. What are other spiritual practices that God uses to keep you close to Him?

SHINE ON!

Father, You love me so well and take such good care of me. Thank You for giving me Scripture and for the faith Your Word gives me. Help me to learn Your promises throughout the Bible. Seal them in my heart so I can know You better and remember Your love always. In the power of Jesus' name. Amen.

Less Bitter, More Glitter

But you are a chosen race, a royal priesthood, a holy nation, a people for His own possession, that you may proclaim the excellencies of Him who called you out of darkness into His marvelous light.

—1 PETER 2:9

Here's how most of us can summarize the decade between ages 10 and 20 years old: "These were the years when I tried to figure out where I belonged."

When you're a little kid, belonging is so obvious. "I belong with my family. I belong at this church. I belong in my class. I belong everywhere."

But then: middle school . . . confusion . . . big changes. As you grow up, you become independent from your family, and you start to understand all the ways you *don't* belong with them.

Your friend group shifts and crashes. You reject the old best friends you loved during the Barbie and make-your-own-slime years. The new you doesn't fit in with them anymore.

Or your former best friend, the one who is suddenly too cool for school (or at least too cool for you), leaves you behind. You're not part of this twosome anymore, so who are you now?

Actually, you also feel like you don't belong in school either. There are all these choices and divisions among kids you have known forever: You're in the AP classes or you're not. You choose band and French, and now you're making all new friends and finding your true passion.

And there are suddenly all of these other changes. You probably never cared if you belonged with boys or at church before. But now your church feels like it's a better fit for your parents. And the boys. Well. THAT is just a hot mess waiting to happen, or that is happening, or that has happened.

So, who are you becoming, and who are your people? In these next pages, we'll look at the messiness that comes with new friend groups, boy drama, and church choices. We'll look for hope in the midst of all the places you feel you don't belong anymore.

Like Peter writes in 1 Peter 2: "You are chosen. You are called out of darkness. You are living in His marvelous light."

This is your truth: You have a deeper, eternal identity than the drama of shifting BFFs, boyfriends, and which math class you're taking. You are God's daughter.

Four Churches Where You Might Belong

~~~~~~~~~~~

Church can be the place where you belong the most: *These are my people. We all believe the same. We love each other, like Jesus told us to love each other.*

Or maybe that's not at all how church feels to you. Maybe it's a painful place where you feel like you should fit in—but you just don't. Isn't church supposed to be a sacred place?

The problem with church is that it's made up of sinners—so there's also gossip, painful fights, egos, and bad ideas. Church can be the messiest place in your life.

The Church is both the Bride of Christ and the place of some people's worst memories or most hurtful seasons.

Throughout your life, you will find yourself embraced by some congregations, as you embrace them as your people. Then, at this same church, you might find yourself feeling like an outsider.

This is just to say that the message of Christ's love delivered to you in the worship service is what you need—but the way it's packaged might be exactly what you don't need.

Here's what you might discover about churches where you feel like you belong (and don't belong).

THE CHURCH OF YOUR GRANDPARENTS

The church of your parents and grandparents (and maybe even great-grandparents) can feel as old and familiar as that worn blanket you carried to day care. Everyone knows you here, including quite a few people you *don't* know. People who changed your diapers now want to tell you about how much you cried in the nursery one Christmas Eve. And this is so awkward.

Why you belong at this church

Everything here is *so familiar*. Hey, look! That altar is the one in all your family's wedding pictures. It's the same scene that's in the background of your grandma's confirmation picture and even of your own Baptism.

This ancient building is in your blood. These weathered pews carry the scent of your earliest memories. So many epic moments have happened under this old steeple that this building feels like God Himself.

Why you don't belong at this church

But sometimes, the shoe (no matter how old and treasured and beautiful) just doesn't fit. It feels too tight or too outdated—or like you're wearing someone else's shoes.

You're ready for a church experience that doesn't feel borrowed, where no one has expectations for who you used to be—and, more important, who you should become. You want a church that belongs to *you*—not the ancient history of your family.

THE CHURCH OF NO TRADITION

This is not your mama's church. This is the church that does everything different, upside down, and in a radically new way. Everyone here is so excited about singing the latest Christian pop songs and doing church in the freshest, most creative ways.

Interpretive dancers? Yes, leaping across the stage. An artist painting during the sermon? He's right there with his watercolors, creating a massive portrait of Jesus. Weekly rock concert—including a five-minute drum solo? Count on it.

You're suddenly experiencing Jesus in new and brilliant ways you didn't know before. And this can feel so thrilling.

Until it's not. Until you're ready for worship to be simple again.

Why you belong at this church

From the design of the building (A circle? This is crazy!) to the cool couches you sit on to worship (Who would have ever thought?), this worship experience is radically different.

Suddenly, your faith feels so new and alive. You love the new music, the daily devotions at Starbucks, and praying with the homeless. This church makes you feel like you're among the very first Christians in the world. You are missionaries in your own city, telling people who never would have stepped into a traditional church all about God.

Why you don't belong at this church

Except sometimes you like tradition and you miss the old ways. You start to question whether everything has to be questioned.

Sometimes you want to hear "Amazing Grace" sung just like it has always been sung. Also, you can't keep up with all the new ideas. Wait. Is Easter service at the beach this year—or are we meeting at the mall? No one seems to know.

Other times you're not sure if the whole couches-in-a-circle layout is the best way to have church. And sometimes there is so much happening that you lose track of the point.

Is the message still about Jesus and His grace? Because it feels like that's gotten lost at your new church.

THE CHURCH THAT IS CONVENIENT

This is the church on the next block over, the one on your college campus, the one where all your friends go, the church where you can be in the award-winning choir, and where they pay you to work in the nursery. This is the church where your dad works, the one connected to your school, the one that has a Saturday night service. This is the church you pass by three times a day anyway—and so you just decide to join it.

This is not—exactly—the church you would pick, but it is the one that's easy. You're busy or going through a hard time or trying to connect with other Christians, and this church works perfectly for all those.

Why you belong at this church

Because it is so easy to show up, and so much of what's happening here is already part of your life. All your friends are in the youth group, or your boyfriend is in the worship band and wants you at every service. No problem. He is so cute when he closes his eyes and totally jams out on the electric guitar.

You're suddenly showing up for every service because this new church is just right there, when you need it. Because of that, you have found a church where you belong.

Why you don't belong at this church

You might also find that the most convenient church is not always the one that works best for you. You get the feeling that when this season of your life is over, you won't be at this church anymore.

You don't totally agree with some of what they say about the Bible, and you don't understand all the history or customs that everyone else seems to get.

But for now, it's the church that works.

THE CHURCH THAT'S BOOMING

Everyone you know goes to this church because there are about a million members—or so it seems. Famous people go here, and so do all your friends. Their events are huge. (An Easter egg hunt for tens of thousands of kids? This is truly madness. News channels outside covering Christmas Eve? Just, wow.) Sunday morning services feel a lot like going to the Super Bowl—stadium and all.

This church is an amazing experience of lights, cameras, and seating for ten thousand. Plus, there's an unbelievable show on the stage (altar?). You will walk away awed because BAM!—this is the church where faith is *happening*.

Why you belong at this church

Every person in your city seems to belong at this church, because there are literally thousands of members. Your pastor has more Twitter followers than a former president.

Your faith feels exciting here. It's like the rock concert of church, and you are showing up and so ready to plug in. Plus, it's handy when you're trying to improve your social life. Thanks to church, you're now hanging at a pool party with the most popular kids at school. You do mission work with NFL players. You just scored an awesome job because the owner of the restaurant goes to this church too.

Why you don't belong at this church

Also, this church can be very loud, chaotic, and a bit impersonal.

On some Sundays, you don't see a single person you know. A man with a purple beard is singing next to you. It would be interesting to ask him about it (since you're members of the same church, singing the same praise song), but he's just as much a stranger as someone you pass on the street. Talking about something as intimate as the hair on his face is too personal.

Isn't church supposed to be a *community* of believers?

Because sometimes this church feels like a crowd of strangers.

GOD'S SILVER (GLITTER) LINING

It feels tricky criticizing church, doesn't it?

Church is where you sing beautiful worship songs, where you hear and better understand God's Word, where you were baptized and confirmed and receive Christ's gifts. It's where you do belong so well.

But it can be pretty devastating when your church family lets you down. When you don't belong, you might even feel like God has let you down.

This is actually a recurring problem for Christians: people at church reject them, and they walk away forever, convinced that God has rejected them. But that's totally the wrong message because God is the one who loves you, who has adopted you. You always belong with God.

This means you can have very high expectations of God's love. His love is eternal, and it will never change, expire, or get tired of you. He never makes mistakes or changes His mind about you. He doesn't get greedy or selfish and snub you. God is the only constant and sure thing in the whole world, and you are part of that world because God planned for you to be born and sent Jesus to rescue you.

Understanding that God loves you can help you see church for what it is—full of sinners who are trying their best to show the world the love of Christ. Sometimes they have ideas that don't work out, or they follow their own plans instead of ones that honor God, or they gossip or fight or judge harshly. This is part of the package of being human: trying to imitate Jesus and getting it wrong lots of times.

Don't give up on church, though. Because here, you can belong with a community of God's children. These are the people who inspire and encourage you as you serve alongside them—even as you do the same for them. This is where you can receive Communion and celebrate Jesus and grow in your faith.

You can shine God's love to those in your church who need to see it.

You can shine His love to the rest of the world, who needs to know that they belong with God.

CONVERSATION SPARKS

1. Church can be a hard place for those who feel like they don't belong. What ways have you seen this to be true? How does sin darken the beauty of church?

2. Look at Hebrews 10:24–25; Matthew 18:20; Colossians 3:16. What does God tell us about church? In your own words, what's the most important part of having a church where you belong?

3. How can you make a difference at your church? List three ways you can help others feel like they belong in God's love.

SHINE ON!

Lord, thank You for Your gift of the Church. You give me friends who encourage and teach me, a pastor who shepherds us, and a place to learn more about You. Help me to live as Your daughter, who loves and forgives and shows up to serve. Let me shine Your light to those who need it—right here in my church and in the world. In Jesus' name. Amen.

Desperate Prayers for Those Who Want to Belong

There are so many different kinds of prayers. There are desperate prayers, serious ones, quick pleas, and long prayer vigils. Jesus tells us in 1 John 5:14 that God hears all these prayers. He wants to hear about all the awkward moments, the cringeworthy situations, and the times that feel like you need miraculous intervention to survive.

You've probably prayed a version of the prayers on these pages. Here's a list of what you might ask God to do in your most unbearable situations of not fitting in.

The prayer from the barbecue, with no one to talk to

Dear Lord, please let me fit in someplace here. I know, I know . . . I fit in with You and Your kingdom and all of that. But to be honest, at this moment, that's not feeling so real. Right now I just need even one person to talk to at this party.

What kind of a barbecue is this anyway? Shouldn't there be games we all have to play? Wouldn't it be better if there was some plan, rather than just standing around and *chatting?* This is an actual nightmare, Lord.

Lord Jesus, I know You talked to the woman at the well when she was feeling out of place. BUT WOW. There are zero people chatting with me over here at the food table. Why did I even come to this ridiculous barbecue? Would it be so bad if I just left? I could stop by later and pick up my jacket from inside, after all these people with friends have gone to do even more fun things together. Surely no one will notice if I just slip away.

If You don't give me someone to talk to in the next ten seconds, I will be the weird girl who just leaves like some kind of a stray animal that wanders in and out of parties.

Thanks, God. You are the literal best.

Amen.

The prayer after seeing the Instagram post of all your friends eating froyo together at YOUR favorite place

Heavenly Father, Creator of everything good, thank You for giving me frozen yogurt, friends, cell phones, and even Instagram. Okay, I need Your help here.

I am so mad at every one of my friends right now. Because apparently, they forgot to send a three-word text that they were meeting for froyo.

Where did they decide to go? To the ONE PLACE that literally everyone knows has my very favorite mochachino frozen yogurt. Not to mention, I am the very person who found this particular froyo place, where they let you play video games while you eat.

Does anyone remember that if it weren't for me, these friends wouldn't be together, playing video games and eating yogurt, Lord? It certainly doesn't seem like they remember that because they absolutely did not text me.

So, give me all Your peace that surpasses understanding to deal with this unfortunate situation. Help me to not worry and obsess that they're probably listing all of my faults right now.

Am I too loud? too shy? dumb? a show-off? Do I stink? Why, oh why, heavenly Father, are they together without me?

I need Your patience, and I need it now.

Amen.

The prayer for Jesus' second coming while eating alone in the school's cafeteria

Please, Lord, let this moment, this horrible lunch, this whole high school existence, be over. Actually, if You could just come back right now, that would be so wonderful. Just go ahead and do the whole Revelation thing right at this second. K? Thanks.

Because I can't do this even one more minute. Why did I sit at this table alone? Why did I choose one with so many chairs so I LOOK so much like I'm sitting alone?

A small table in the corner, Lord. That would have worked beautifully. I could have pulled out some homework. I could have pretended like I needed to sit by myself. A small table in the corner would have been a million times better than sitting here—so obviously—in the middle of the cafeteria by *myself*.

Oh, thank You, God. Yes, this girl, right now. She is the one! Thanks for sending me a new friend! All those assemblies about kindness and not bullying are working. She looks nice, like she might have lots of friends. I'm so glad I chose this big table!

But no. What is she saying about needing to borrow these chairs? No! Quick! A miracle. Make her sit in one of the chairs! This is a tiny miracle, God. It's not like parting a sea or healing anyone. JUST MAKE HER SIT.

Okay, so she's taking a couple of the chairs. Maybe this is good, God? Maybe it will look like I'm doing some sort of job at this table and that's why I'm sitting here? I am the official Chair Keeper? Or selling them or something? Make everyone who is staring believe that, God. Like now. Please.

Or You could always just send Jesus back. This second. Seriously. This very instant is the moment that would work best for me.

Thanks.

(Still waiting, Lord.)

Amen.

The prayer for a boyfriend/a friend that's a boy/a boy who likes me

Heavenly Father, You know what the future holds, who I'll marry, and even how I'll wear my hair as I walk down the aisle to begin my life with my future soul mate.

I'm not asking You to reveal who that guy is or what color his eyes are. I just need a tiny favor here.

Please, Holy Spirit, could You nudge the heart of just one boy to think I'm pretty? Just one guy who will smile at me and let me know that I am not completely weird or unattractive or have terrible breath?

How about we compromise with a cute boy to text me? That's all I want. And maybe we could just kind of hang out at the mall on some Saturday afternoons or go to funny movies together. Just a boy who is always there for school dances or group projects, when everyone else is pairing up.

I promise to worship only You, God—even if the boy You send is very sweet and thinks I'm wonderful.

Thanks! Amen.

The prayer for a best friend who loves me unconditionally forever and ever

Dear God, Jesus, the Holy Spirit. All of You, please help. I need a true best friend, like a capital B-F-F. I am so ready to have someone who belongs to me and cares about me—even when I'm grouchy or boring. I need someone whom I can really trust to keep all my secrets.

I need to be part of a twosome, like I see on Disney shows. I really, really want a forever friend, who is the salt to my pepper, the peas to my carrots, the one who listens to my weird stories.

I'm counting on You, dear Jesus, to come through with a BFF who is funny and sweet and sporty and loyal and never gets annoyed with me. Please, combine all of that together for the whole package of a friend so I never have to be lonely again. We will take road trips together and have hundreds of sleepovers, and we will always have each other's backs.

Also, could You send her now so we can get busy on making a lifetime of memories and inside jokes? I'm ready to know my future college roommate, my maid of honor, the godmother to my future babies.

(And yes, I know You are the best Friend a girl could ask for, but thanks for giving me one here too.)

Amen.

GOD'S SILVER (GLITTER) LINING

Okay, yes, these prayers are ridiculous—and also so true. We've all found ourselves in the situation of terrible awkwardness and the desperate need to belong.

In fact (and this is the irony), this is the group where we all *do* belong. Every person has felt the pain of being excluded, the desperation of wanting to belong, and the frustration of being left behind.

This is a dreadful club to belong to because our need for acceptance—to feel liked—is one of our most basic needs. When that need isn't met, we start shooting arrow prayers at God to fix it *right now*.

The truth is bittersweet: we will never feel totally accepted in this world—and that's okay. Because in this world, it's humans doing the accepting, and we're full of sin and hurt and jealousy and anger. Even the way we accept one another is flawed. The best BFF will let you down, the boy who likes you may also confuse you, and the group that accepts you can turn on you.

But the good news is that you are truly home with Jesus. So, even when this world is awkward and hard, your perfect Savior is always listening, always helping, always accepting.

CONVERSATION SPARKS

1. Tell your story about your desperate need to belong. What prayers have you said when you felt like you needed a miracle to fit in? How has God answered your prayers?

2. In your own words, how has God already answered your prayer by giving you Jesus and fulfilling your deepest need to belong?

3. Read 1 John 2. What do we learn about how to love others?

SHINE ON!

Dear heavenly Father, thank You for hearing all my desperate prayers. I am so grateful for all my friends and family, and for the beautiful chances You've given me to belong in this world. More than anything, Lord, thank You for sending Your Son, Jesus, so I can belong as Your daughter forever and ever. In His name. Amen.

Southern Sororities, Not Belonging, and the Scars of High School

Let me be clear that sororities in high school are a terrible idea. Like, truly among the worst ideas ever. The Greek system is like steroids to cliques—and in high school, cliques don't need encouragement.

Plus, many of the social activities for fraternities and sororities revolve around underage drinking (like the kind of reckless binge drinking that makes headlines). Then there's hazing—it's illegal, and when mean girls set the rules, it can be dangerous.

Yet at my high school, sororities ruled the social stratosphere. The repercussions and rejections of that are still part of me today. Do I know what I'm talking about when it comes to not belonging? Yes, I do. I still have the scars.

I grew up in the Deep South, in Galveston, a small island city off the coast of Texas. Among the families was a caste system—either they were old money or living in poverty.

Our family was different. My parents had both come to Galveston to teach at the Lutheran school connected to our church. My brother and I were at that school for our elementary years—the exact years when the other kids were figuring out friendships and alliances. We were teachers' kids, neither rich nor poor, and raised separate from the Galveston society families. And so, when I did join the other kids at our local public school, I was so eager to fit in.

At first, it seemed like good news that our high school had sororities. This system felt like a trustworthy method for finding my people and really, finally, belonging. I took huge comfort in the promise that membership in the sorority would guarantee real friends.

Like a fairy garden, I could instantly construct an entire social world around me. Of the four sororities and two fraternities, most of them had been around so long that my classmates were the second or third generation to join. Instead of prom, there were elaborate debutante formals. The fraternities and sororities hosted these over-the-top balls. All the school's social activities centered around the parties the Greek system had on the weekends. Acceptance into this society meant instant social success.

Right before my freshman year, I received an invite to the mother/daughter rush party for the sorority I most wanted to join. Some girls were invited to rush parties for all the sororities, but I wasn't greedy. I just needed one sisterhood to invite me to join their ranks.

The rush party was a make-it-or-break-it kind of event. All I had to do was impress the members, and they would vote to allow me to pledge. This moment would mean crossing a bridge from Girl with Potential to Girl Who Belongs. Joining this one sorority was my winning lottery ticket, my paved future, my promised land. This would be freedom from awkwardness and social insecurity.

I gave a lot of thought to the actual party. What would we do? What would bring my success? Should I be the version of myself that's loud and funny and gets a lot of attention? Or the one that's quiet and serious and follows the rules?

Because, yes, everyone says to "just be yourself," but let's be honest. *Yourself* can have hundreds of different shadings and modes. Which one belonged with this sorority? I would become that girl.

The tea party itself was grueling. My mom and I didn't know anyone. And to be clear, a rush party is all about showcasing your popularity—so you can attract the attention of the sorority members. I planned to work the crowd like a politician, but I couldn't find anyone who looked as out of place as I felt. A haunted house would have been less terrifying than this house, with one shiny sorority girl after another laughing and talking and being generally fabulous. Two hours later, I went home—exhausted and anxious—to await my social fate.

I learned later what happened after the rush party: the members kicked off their heels, grabbed snacks and leftover cans of Coke, and met for hours in the living room. Here, they drafted their future friends, like NFL coaches pick their teams. They discussed the freshmen and rated their beauty, popularity, and personalities. Then they voted over each girl, confident with the superiority that comes from judging who is worthy of your friendship.

After the voting, when the upperclassmen had chosen the lucky twelve freshmen, they created fancy invitations for each of the prospective pledges. They also gathered elaborate bouquets of flowers, balloons, and confetti to bring to the chosen dozen. The sorority sisters decorated their cars and headed out in packs to invite the New Pledges. They caravanned around our small island, honking and screaming from their decorated cars.

All over Galveston, freshmen girls were peeking out of their windows and praying. Each of us was desperately hoping for an invite from one of the sororities, like little kids waiting for Santa. I learned later that every single one of us felt the same that night: insecure, scared, and so hopeful. Would the older girls come, handing out flowers and balloons, giving us an invitation into the secret society of partying, dressing up, dating, and instant friends? Would the invitation come—to *belong*?

My invitation didn't come that night. I waited at the window, and then in my room, and then finally in my bed—under my covers, straining to hear the honks of the sorority sisters. That night still stands out in my personal history as one of the hardest of not belonging.

For the next four years, I lived with the sting of that rejection. To cover my hurt, I often told people that I had chosen not to pledge. I didn't want to admit the truth—that I wasn't actually asked.

I can see now that I was way too insecure and needy for sorority life. I would have gotten caught up with drinking and parties and everything I didn't need. I was too vulnerable. I would later come to understand that God was protecting me from these temptations.

But when I was fourteen? I had prayed hard that I would be asked to be part of exactly this. I needed the membership card and guaranteed friends to feel secure. Even at the end of high school, when I had much more confidence and a better understanding of who I was, I was still envious of the easy sisterhood the members of those sororities shared.

GOD'S SILVER (GLITTER) LINING

Here is the truth about belonging: sometimes you totally don't. You don't make the team or choir or band. Your boyfriend tells you that he likes someone else and not to text him anymore. You never get invited to join the club, or your teacher tells you to change your schedule because you're not cutting it in AP classes.

These are such clear turning points in your life that you might wonder what could have happened had you gotten what you wanted. Yes, the rejection hurts. But there's usually more to the story. God's protection is often wrapped up in it.

Maybe the sorority isn't the best way for you to spend your high school years, and so you don't get the engraved invitation to join. Or this boy will continue to grow impatient with you for not having sex, and you will have to keep fighting with him about it, and he will break up with you. That will turn out to be good news. Or maybe choir isn't your thing because the Earth Club needs your voice. Or you don't get the lead in the play because a friend needs you during the same season you would have been learning lines at late-night rehearsals.

We learn these lessons kind of blindly. They all feel like rejection and failure at first. But as your story keeps unfolding, you keep learning about more and more ways that God is providing for you and protecting you. You start to trust that if you pray for something and you work for it and God still says no, then it wasn't in His plan for you.

The deeper lesson here is learning that this change in your story doesn't define you. Maybe you didn't find the perfect group of friends this semester, but God might have a group right around the corner that will be your secret keepers, your partners in silliness, and your encouragers. Don't give up on them yet—you have time.

Most of all, remember that your most important acceptance is with your Savior. That is the identity to cling to when it feels like a social rejection might define you. Everything else is so temporary; your status as His daughter is eternal.

Shine that identity to the world.

CONVERSATION SPARKS

1. Tell a story about a time God said no and you discovered His protection in that.

2. What prayer to belong do you have right now? Tell the group (or write here) about one place where you hope to belong–either a team or a club or a college you want to accept you.

3. Read Deuteronomy 31:6. Talk about the promise in this verse. What would this have meant for God's people in the Old Testament? What does it mean for you now?

SHINE ON!

Dear heavenly Father, You provide for me and protect me in the most important ways. Keep me close to You always, Lord. Anchor my identity in You, deep in my soul. In Jesus' name. Amen.

Seven Lessons You Learn from Bad Boyfriends

*(A Spiritual Wellness Guide to Spare You
from the Worst Relationship Dumpster Fires)*

Lesson 1: Your worst fears about boyfriends will most likely come true. (Sorry.)

The bad news first: the hardest heartbreaks probably will happen to you.

These are the breakups when you find out your boyfriend has been texting another girl. Or you realize that the one you thought you would love forever is actually the one you're arguing with every single day.

Or when the boyfriend who pays extra attention to you and gives you extra advice about how to dress and wear your hair is also extra interested in you not talking to your friends, and then turns out to be an extra-special control freak who won't let you break up with him.

Or you become the only person your tortured-soul boyfriend will listen to when he thinks he needs to smoke weed or drink a six-pack of beer to relax.

During these years, you're learning so much about yourself and love and boys in general. But you haven't yet learned *these* lessons. And learning them can be the very hardest seasons of your young life.

Dating during your teen years is like learning to ride a unicycle. You keep trying to lean on support that isn't there. You haven't developed the stronger muscles of trust in God (but you will). You keep tipping over and collecting bruises and scrapes and (sometimes) deep scars.

As it turns out, the bruises and the scrapes—and even the scars—will be how you learn the lessons. Love your Savior, love yourself, and understand that you have your whole life to fall in love.

When the drama hits (and it will hit), you will need a place to go to know you're okay. You're not defined by this heartbreak and disappointment. You are defined by your Savior, who tells you that you belong to Him. He has claimed you, and this terrible the-bottom-has-fallen-out-of-my-life drama cannot change that.

Lesson 2: The more you need to be loved, the harder you are to love.

Look, this truth is problematic and annoying.

If I were God, I would design relationships to function much more like Amazon Prime: need it, find it in another person, claim it, have it forever.

Unfortunately, this is just about the opposite of how relationships work—especially with boys and most especially when you're a teenager. Instead, the more you need, say, a boy to tell you that you're pretty, the more complicated that becomes. You will end up dating a boy who never tells you you're pretty. Or you will end up dating a mean one who tells you that you're prettiest when you're doing exactly what he wants.

Or the more you need a boyfriend to feel complete, the more you date bad boyfriends who keep dumping you. Or the harder it is to get anyone to like you.

This feels like a terrible system. I have no idea why it works this way.

Okay, I do have a small idea. I think it's because neediness is so exhausting to be around. If you're needy for boys to approve of you, they can sniff it out like bad perfume. It attracts all the wrong people and things. It repels the good relationships. Also this kind of neediness is making yourself into your own god. Instead of trusting Him or following His commandments, your own need to belong is the most important part of your life.

This is a painful truth that takes decades to learn. So I'm giving you the secret right here. Love the person God has made you to be. Love her like she is a precious creation by the Master of the universe. Love her like you are important enough for Jesus Himself to come to earth and die for you.

Because you absolutely are.

Lesson 3: You are so very beautiful. You just are. Truly.

Don't come at me with your "Except my thighs" or "I hate my nose/eyebrows/belly/short legs." Just stop.

The first reason to stop pointing out your flaws is that it's exhausting. Everyone gets tired of insisting, "No, really, your head does not look like a potato." The truth is, we all have about ten seconds of patience for conversations about your bad hair.

Next, it's time to believe that God is the best artist in the universe, and He knows what He's doing. You look exactly like you're supposed to look. This is your version of beautiful, and it's exactly right for you. #sorrynotsorry. #stopinsultingHiscreation

Those thick arms you want to cover up might be the perfect ones for lifting patients when you're an EMT medic. Your pointy chin is from your grandma, and when she's gone, you will still see a little of her face, right on the tip of yours. One day, your chin might become your favorite body part.

The sooner you make peace with your body being the exact creation that God intended—and loving it as His masterpiece—the sooner the rest of the world will see it like that too.

From now on, ask God to help you with this. Make a promise to be a good steward of your body—to feed it well and treat it well and keep harmful substances out of it. Make a promise to never call yourself ugly just so a boy will tell you that you're wrong.

Instead, believe you are beautiful.

Because you totally are.

Lesson 4: Pictures are permanent records.

You probably already know that your school permanent record is a big deal. If you cut off your friend's braids in kindergarten, your teacher will record this offense in your permanent record, and this crime will follow you around until you're twenty-six and working on your PhD. Or if you cheat on your ninth-grade history test, the principal might decide this crime should keep you out of Harvard.

As a driver, you also have a permanent record. If you run a few stop signs and forget to slow down in school zones, the police will ticket you, and these offenses will follow you around. If you accumulate enough of them, the courts will decide you would be better off riding a bike and take away your license.

Here's the bad news about permanent records. They never seem to record your good deeds. No one ever writes that you're a wonderful young lady who has taken hundreds of tests and not cheated. The Department of Motor Vehicles doesn't note that you always let other drivers merge into your lane and you never look at your phone when you're driving and you wear your seat belt like a champ.

Pictures are like your permanent record. You will take thousands of selfies and snaps in your life. Most of them will be nice photos of your new haircut or of you helping your little brother bake muffins.

But there will also be the chance to take inappropriate pictures. This comes when your crush "dares" you to text him a picture of you lying in bed in your tight white tank top.

Or your friends want to post pictures of you in your bikini making kissy faces at the camera. Why not? Your Instagram feed is a constant stream of pictures just like this one. And oh, the "likes" you'll get.

But here's the deal about pictures: they follow you around like a speeding ticket or bad decision in kindergarten. A snapshot seems so innocent, so quick, so forgettable.

Except the whole appeal of pictures is just the opposite of that. They're permanent. They're a record that follows you around. That sexy selfie now lives on the phone of a guy who can use it however he wants.

Keep your picture record clear. Stay out of the ones you don't want following you around when you're thirty. You will be *so over* that boy who broke your heart—but he still has your scandalous picture on his phone.

Lesson 5: Perfect Boys exist only in books.

I write young adult novels, so I spend hours every day inventing The Perfect Boy. This figment-of-my-imagination stud has a sharp wit, mesmerizing eyes, wisdom beyond his years, and a deep sense of right and wrong, and he saves stray dogs. He is athletic and Christian, and he serves his community and easily gets into his dream college. He also has plenty of time for a job and to daydream about the quirky but beautiful girl he loves.

The Perfect Boy is a fairy tale—yet he is so irresistible that many of us make him our standard for falling in love. We decide that life begins only when we meet our own version of The Perfect Boy. We believe these lies: "If only this boy loved me, I could sparkle." "I am beautiful only through his eyes." "He would complete me."

These lies set up a losing game because perfect humans exist only in fiction.

Searching for The Perfect Boy is all about our human need for our Savior. Your soul has a God-size hole that needs Jesus (your actual Savior) to fill it. Fairy tales will tell us that marrying Prince Charming will make all our dreams come true, but that's just not true.

Every single person—including the boy with the broad shoulders, nice car, and cute jokes—is also full of flaws and sin and bad habits and confusion. At some point, you have to lower your expectations of real-life boys.

Instead, learn more about your Savior, who is real and who does love you completely and perfectly. I promise that He will never let you down.

Lesson 6: You can't go back to holding hands.

You've probably heard the crude comparison of making out with your boyfriend and the bases in baseball. First base is kissing; second base is touching in the bathing-suit area; third base is clothes off; and a home run is sex.

Yuck. I know. So tacky. The person who first thought of the baseball comparison didn't understand that sex is beautiful, created by God, and created for marriage.

Or maybe that's the truth in this analogy because making out is like baseball in one way: When you're a base runner, you're trying to score a run. You make it to second base, and you're already looking ahead to third base. You're wondering how you can steal or get batted to the next stop on your quest to get home.

When you start making out with your boyfriend, it feels like this. Progress is getting to the next base. As in baseball, once you're on second, you're not thinking about walking back to first base.

You'll probably tell yourself that you can go back to holding hands at any time, but that's never how it works. You're right back on second base every time you start kissing. There's also a powerful sense of belonging that comes with making out. Your boyfriend seems to need this. He wants time with only you so badly. He's so focused on your shared goal of progressing to the next base.

But this is a losing game because you're getting closer and closer to where you don't want to be. And you can't go back to holding hands.

Understand this truth so that you can set realistic rules early on. God is so very clear that all these stages leading up to sex should be part of marriage only.

Your Creator, who designed you and understands you in an eternal way, knows that going too far too early will put you in a physical place that He designed for husbands and wives.

And you can't go back to holding hands.

Lesson 7: Don't have sex until you're married.

Or if you're already having sex, stop now.

Yes, you can absolutely make this decision. Don't tell me that staying a virgin is unrealistic. I don't believe that teens are helpless about their sexual desires. If you were diabetic, you wouldn't eat sugar. If you have tree allergies, you don't go outside in the spring. You don't touch the hot stove. You don't text while driving, and you wear your seat belt. You are capable of changing your behaviors to avoid what's not good for you.

Also, the peer pressure thing is not a good argument. Because here's the truth: everyone who is pressuring you to have sex (your boyfriend, your friends, society in general) wants you to do this because it benefits them.

Your best friend feels guilty about the sex she's having, and it would relieve some of her guilt if you were too. Your crush has decided he cannot control his sexual desires and needs you to be his accomplice in giving in to them. Books and movies have glorified teen sex because it sells books and movies.

This is so messed up because sex is all about intimacy and a very private connection between husbands and wives. Why does Hollywood get a say in that? Why does your best friend get to tell you how to use your body? Why does your boyfriend at sixteen get to take something from you that should be reserved for your husband—whom you will love so much more and for forever?

These people do not get a say—unless you let them.

Decide now that God is right about this and save the intimacy and connection of sex for your husband. The Sixth Commandment ("You shall not commit adultery") is about loving and honoring your spouse with your body. You're not married yet, but not having sex now honors the one you will love forever.

You will not regret it.

GOD'S SILVER (GLITTER) LINING

Raise your hand if your definition of belonging includes a boy.

You probably believe what most of us do: You will feel truly accepted when the right guy loves you. In some way, this will solve all your problems. Your love story with him will cover all your insecurities. He will fill you up with the kind of belonging you have always needed.

Of course, you believe this; the media constantly sells this story of true acceptance. The wedding industry, happily-ever-after movies, and ads you have to watch before your favorite YouTube video are all about finding Mr. Right and becoming half of a twosome. Then, of course, you will live in bliss.

This lie really does lead to the worst dumpster fires in relationships. Awful breakups, ugly fights, sex before marriage, terrible (soul-deep) pain, shame, and guilt—these are all part of the pain of bad relationships.

Your insecurity and your neediness are the gasoline you keep pouring on these disastrous relationships.

You can't avoid all of the awkwardness and pain that comes with dating, but for your part, you can come to your relationships whole in your Savior.

Here's what that looks like: Believe that the true love you need comes from your heavenly Father. Love His creation in you. Cling to His promise to provide for you. Feel this security of Christ deep inside your soul. Return again and again to God's promises—in His Word, in Holy Communion. Pray for the Holy Spirit to saturate your whole being with His acceptance.

Trust me on this. God gave His Son so you would know these lessons and so you can live them out. The women who have gone through adolescence before you are cheering you on to know you are loved and secure. We want better for you than what this messed-up world can offer. That's our prayer for you.

May you shine God's love into the darkness and confusion that comes with early love. May He bless you with easy lessons, kind boyfriends, and the deep understanding that you already belong in the most important ways.

Go forth and shine, beautiful one. God is with you.

CONVERSATION SPARKS

1. With one word, describe your history with boyfriends so far. Have you had a bad relationship? good relationship? no relationship?

2. Read Matthew 6:21–23. Talk about Jesus' words here. What is the "eye" He is teaching about? What is the "darkness"? How does this relate to boyfriends?

3. Write yourself a letter about what it means to be fully accepted by God, to belong with Him forever. Give yourself dating advice. Take a picture of that letter and keep it on your phone. Refer to it during every season when you find yourself in a bad place with boys. You can also share your thoughts with the group.

SHINE ON!

Lord, You are the one who fills up my soul. You love me with the deepest love, in exactly the perfect ways. Seal this confidence in my soul, dear God. Let me believe this. Help me to know this every minute of every day. Protect me in every relationship and keep me close to You through Your Holy Spirit. In Jesus' name. Amen.

Let It Glow!

*In the same way, let your light shine before
others, so that they may see your good works and
give glory to your Father who is in heaven.*

—MATTHEW 5:16

Long, long ago (around the year 2000), the world was a very dark place.

No one had cell phones, and so we all had to carry flashlights in our cars, on our keychains, in our purses, and even in our pockets.

Sometimes you would find yourself in a dark situation with no way to see at all. Maybe you came home after a movie and your porch light was burned out. Or perhaps you had to walk to your car in a desolate parking lot—and then you dropped your keys. You were just out of luck, crawling around on the black asphalt, totally lost . . . unless someone came by with one of those keychain flashlights.

In the past decade, cell phones have changed our lives so dramatically that we almost can't imagine life without them. Even though we have hundreds of uses for our phones (prom dress apps, FaceTiming, snaps, carrying around ALL OUR RECORDED MUSIC), they also serve as very convenient flashlights.

Without the millions of beams of light provided by our phones, many of us would be lost. When the electricity goes out in a stadium, everyone reaches for their cell phones—not to call for help, but so they can see again. When you wake up in the middle of the night, you stumble through your dark bedroom by the light of your phone. When you drop your charger behind the dresser, you use your phone's last juice to shine its light back there.

In the history of light, cell phones have been one of the most magnificent inventions—little beams in every pocket for everyone and everywhere.

Light hasn't always been this convenient, though. When Jesus tells the crowd in Matthew 5 to be the light of the world, He is talking to a group who knew real darkness: people who had light from only a candle or lamp . . . those with no streetlights . . . buildings and homes with no fluorescent lights or convenient undercounter LED lights.

Jesus tells this crowd on the mountain: "You are the light of the world. A city set on a hill cannot be hidden. Nor do people light a lamp and put it under a basket, but on a stand, and it gives light to all in the house. In the same way, let your light shine before others, so that they may see your good works and give glory to your Father who is in heaven" (Matthew 5:14–16).

Jesus uses this light metaphor to a crowd of people who knew very well how dangerous it is to stumble around in the darkness. He points out that if you have light—something that can help so many people—then BY ALL MEANS share it.

Put that light on a stand, Jesus tells the crowd. "Let it give light to everyone in the house." Also, do this with your good works, Jesus tells them. Serve the world—so everyone can clearly see who God is.

This is the charge that Jesus gives to you and me too. Thanks to God's great love for us, we know real peace. If we have this security—something that can help so many people—then BY ALL MEANS share it with everyone. Share it by serving. Sparkle, shine, and show the world who God is.

Because, as we understand by reading the Bible, the world will know the love of God by the way we reflect His love in real ways. They will know that God loves them by the way you take care of them in His name. Friends will know God's care by the way you share food with them. Your family will understand Jesus' sacrifice by the way you forgive them over and over again. Your church family will know your Father's faithfulness by the loyal way you show up to help with worship.

The world doesn't have to be dark—we have the light, and it is the command, the invitation, and the great pleasure of our Savior for us to share that light with the world.

Sparkle, shine, and show the world God's love.

The Flood and the Football Players

These are the two most important truths about our city of Katy, Texas: we are very good at building, and we are very good at football.

For the football part, there are state and national wins to prove our city's fame. Our football team has beaten every other football team in the state. They've actually won more than any other high school team in the nation. (Okay, here is where the really die-hard fans would want me to mention we are actually the *world* champions of high school football. The champions of the entire *galaxy*.) When Texans talk football, it quickly escalates to galaxy-level competitions.

To become this good at football, families start training their kids young. Boys suit up in shoulder pads and cleats before they're in kindergarten. And we don't grow just football players here in Katy. Girls are preened at the most competitive cheerleading clinics. By the time these athletes reach high school, they've been groomed to be the best.

The practices themselves are impressive. Athletes here practice every day—sometimes twice a day—to become the toughest, fastest, strongest, and smartest. They practice in 100-degree heat. Soccer players run in the rain, even in the off-season. Volleyball players and swimmers and sprinters begin their training before dawn and are still at it well after sunset.

But in a city of shining athletes, it's the football players who shimmer as the local celebrities. Case in point: A couple of years ago, in early November, I was enjoying a bowl of broccoli cheddar soup at our local Panera. At the table next to me was a group of older men who were discussing the district finals of the Katy High School football team. They talked with so much passion, they sounded like generals drawing up battle plans or oil executives strategizing a company takeover.

It's hard not to feel cynical about football in a city so in love with it. As I ate my soup, I wanted to laugh. These boys were young enough to be their grandchildren. And yet, these old guys were talking about them like they were celebrities.

Then, suddenly, those very Tigers—the Katy High School defensive line—walked into Panera after their Saturday morning practice. The men at that table stood and swooned as if Taylor Swift herself had walked into a Justice store. They pulled out chairs for the boys. One man sprinted to the counter to get them smoothies.

The football players handled the men's praise easily. They were used to being heroes. After all, they were football players in Katy, the city that just built a $75 million stadium for our high school football players.

This is our city's other obsession: building very shiny new buildings. For the ten years our family has lived in Katy, the city has sprawled. Entire neighborhoods seem to pop up overnight, and homes sprout from the ground like weeds. These houses boast theater rooms and sparkling swimming pools. The neighborhoods have miles of walking trails and kids' parks that look like space stations. The map app on my phone doesn't even know about most of these neighborhoods. They're that new.

But times change. Katy wasn't always covered in new houses that held spectacular athletes. A hundred years ago, farmers made a good living growing rice for the rest of the country. Rice crops grew so well here because our soil is mostly clay and it holds in moisture. Clay soil shifts and molds to the shallow root system of rice plants. Remember this about our soil because, as you will see, it will mean bad news for all those new houses.

In August 2017, our high school football teams were just getting ready for their first games of the season. That same week, meteorologists were getting nervous about a hurricane named Harvey that was gaining strength in the Gulf of Mexico. The newscasters called the storm a "rainmaker," but no one else paid much attention.

Then, on August 26, Harvey made landfall in Texas, and you probably heard the rest of the story. Fifty inches of rain in three days. To any city, this would be catastrophic, but to a city with so many new houses, on so much clay soil, this amount of rain was deadly.

Families watched the water rise until they were forced to their roofs. When the rain spilled through the windows of our dear friends' home, they strapped floaties on their young sons and waded through chest-high water to safety. They lost their house and nearly everything in it.

When the rain finally stopped, chaos fell on our city. First responders couldn't reach all the people trapped in their island homes. The tension was high. Most stores and roads were closed. Hospitals were overflowing with people needing help. When a grocery store opened its doors for a few hours, a fistfight broke out in line.

But then, thanks to social media, ragtag plans quickly came together. Churches organized food banks and delivered busloads of toilet paper, bottled water, towels, and generators. Families and their pets camped out in schools that had not flooded. Teachers worked tirelessly to pass out potato chips and Pop-Tarts to stranded families.

But for me—for most of us—it was the high school football players who became the heroes we would never forget. These young men, who had trained in the worst conditions of hot and humid Katy, Texas, were the ones who knew how to show up and get a job done.

These athletes had learned at a young age to work as a team. They were well suited for the job of moving out soggy couches, ripping up moldy carpet, and hauling out waterlogged appliances. They carried out boxes of ruined family photo albums and kids' artwork and spread it out on the grass to dry in the Texas sun. And they did it all with a smile.

One friend told me that the football team from Katy High School—those same Tigers who had been at Panera—came into her flooded house and tore out the wet walls with sledgehammers. Ten of them did the work of fifty. They were finished in two hours.

Of all these heroic stories, the one that sticks with me most is the one about a football player named Tommy and his teammates who walked into a terrible situation on the outskirts of Katy. This was not in one of the shiny new neighborhoods—this is where the older homes are.

For five days, the floodwaters had kept a mom and her three kids stuck inside their home. They were running out of food. The carpet and couches were soaked, and the stench of mold was gagging. Tommy and his buddies came in and ransacked the place. They moved what they could to the second floor of the house and set up a makeshift living situation for the mom and those kids. They hauled out everything wet, then contacted the local churches about what the family still needed. Then Tommy led the team and they bent down on their knees and prayed with the family—just like their coach had prayed with them before every game. Tommy told the family, "This is God. He's helping you. We're showing up for Him."

The stories of Katy's football players and soccer teams and volleyball players helping people were all over the news. Cheerleading squads reached out to other groups across the country. Schools from Minnesota, Maine, and Montana sent Home Depot and Walmart gift cards so people could buy necessities. Basketball teams met together to deliver meals to first responders.

These athletes mucked out an unbelievable number of homes. The number is in the thousands. A soccer player created T-shirts with Psalm 46:1, "God is our refuge and strength, a very present help in trouble," and sold them online, donating the profits to Harvey relief. When the adults didn't know what to do, these athletes came in and took care of business.

To be clear, many, many people helped Katy recover from Hurricane Harvey. Every family has a story about helping or being helped. Youth groups and whole congregations also mucked out houses and organized donations and delivered supplies. But the athletes had been trained to help in a way that was different from any other. They knew how to think quickly, how to deal with tough circumstances, how to trust one another, and how to work under pressure in difficult conditions.

Although I wasn't an athlete in high school, I learned a lot about training by watching the way those teams helped. Those young men and women had been training all these years, and their training paid off. When tragedy struck our city, these high school athletes really were the heroes.

GOD'S SILVER (GLITTER) LINING

What about you? What are you training for? Because it matters. The way you spend your time and energy adds up to something. What influences are you welcoming into your life? What people or ideas are you allowing to shape your character?

As you've probably learned, life twists on hairpin turns. You never know when you'll have the chance to help, to share what you've learned, to shine love to someone, to share your faith. Maybe it will be after a hurricane or a fire or tornado in your own hometown. Or maybe it will be when someone you love needs to hear the truth of her Savior.

All the time, God is equipping you for this. He wants you to be so sure of His love that you can share it with the world.

CONVERSATION SPARKS

1. Talk about your history with sports. Have you trained as an athlete? How has this changed you? What other training have you received? Have you trained hard as a student? a musician? an actress? How has this preparation formed and changed you?

2. Read 2 Timothy 3:16-17. What does this say about training? How has the Bible helped to train you to understand God's love?

3. In your faith life, what has been the most helpful training? Sunday School? Confirmation? A retreat or mission
trip? Be specific here. Write down (or tell the group)
ways God has trained you to share His love with the
world. Has He given you specific friends or leaders who
have inspired or encouraged you? How has the Bible
helped you? Which specific verses?

SHINE ON

Lord, You are the one who gives perfect training. You teach me about
Your love and send me out to share it with those who need it. Thanks
for caring for me in every single way and for showing me ways to
care for others. Help me to love the world in Your name, Lord. Amen.

How to Find Your Thing

1. You really need a thing.

Somewhere out there, there is a volleyball team that needs its star setter . . . a nonprofit waiting for its founder . . . a clothing line desperate for its designer . . . an invention that will wipe global warming (or JoJo Siwa songs) right off the face of the earth.

If God's not going to send you an engraved invitation announcing your mission in life on your eleventh birthday, then you will have to go find it yourself.

The only solution here is to dive into ALL THE ACTIVITIES.

From this day forward, you will be laser-focused on discovering this very specific task that God has set out for you. Yes, you will have to invest all your time and energy into searching for your thing, but you are diligent.

Lie in bed at night and deliver long lectures to God about stepping up His hints here to show you exactly what your life purpose is.

2. Try EVERYTHING.

Swim team in the summer, soccer in the fall, basketball through the winter, and track in the spring (plus a little church softball and a weekend archery retreat, for fun).

And that's just the sports.

Join a quilting club. Shoot vlogs every night for your newly launched YouTube channel where you broadcast the daily news from your life. Buy a sewing machine and ten yards of sequined material to make your own line of signature T-shirts. Start a nonprofit called OreoButter for Old-Timers; then convince your youth group that you should make your own cookie butter and donate the profits to the nursing home.

You are unstoppable. Yes, a tiny bit too busy. But it's fine! No more sitting around, watching every other girl find her thing.

Now *you* are the trendsetter. And it feels fabulous.

(Also, *so exhausting.*)

3. You are in (literal) pain.

Okay, so it turns out you might not be cut out for sports. Or at least not this many sports.

You break your nose in the freestyle relay, which even your coach has never heard of before. But really? Shouldn't someone have warned you that the end of the pool was RIGHT THERE?

Then there was the concussion during soccer. It was just a terrible coincidence that your head was exactly where that girl's foot landed when she tried to kick the ball to China.

And yes, you were the only player in the history of basketball who needed to wear a borrowed football helmet, but your mom wasn't going to let you risk any more head injuries after the soccer concussion. The helmet did protect your head—even though it didn't help you see the basket. This explains that awkward moment when you scored the (winning) two points for the other team.

At least track season went well. Except for that unfortunate realization that the shot put is so much heavier than it looks. Also, wow . . . throwing it farther than two feet is actually impossible.

4. Stop. Rewind. *THIS* is your thing.

Not everyone is an athlete, which is why you are so excited that you are killing it with your T-shirt business. Who would have thought so many of your little sister's friends would love the sequined pink T-shirts?

You are a born entrepreneur with a natural sense for making money. You have thirty-seven orders before you've even started sewing. Imagine when these girls start wearing your creations and tagging you with the most brilliant hashtag ever: #p!nkit!

Except the sewing machine is giving you a hard time with the weird bobbin thing and *all this thread*. What is this madness? Has no one invented a better way to sew after all these centuries? Are we still making shirts with hundreds of individual stitches? How does Gap make billions of shirts every day? Surely there's a better system for this because you do not have the patience for archaic hobbies like this terrible sewing.

You do have a talent for one hobby: baking. Or rather, *blending* Oreos—and creating the most delicious cookie butter ever. You and your youth group friends have learned you just have to toss a package of Oreos into the blender, and it will magically become cookies-and-cream delight.

Fill thirty-two mason jars with the creamiest, chocolatiest, ooey-gooey goodness. Reward your #missionteam by letting them eat a couple of jars, and then eat an entire jar yourself because you are a generous person who deserves delicious splurges in her life.

Feel sick—and even sicker when someone rants about you on Instagram for calling residents at the nursing home "old-timers."

Defend yourself by explaining that you are doing a thing with the title—and OreoButter for the Elderly doesn't have the same ring.

But you lose the online war when the internet troll screenshots your reply and shares it as a rant that "ageism is the OLDEST form of prejudice and the problem with this world!"

This post gets more than a hundred likes, and the makers of Oreo cookies even tweet that their company is in no way connected to you or your "attempt to shame the greatest generation this country has ever known."

5. Drama, drama, drama. (Maybe THAT is your thing?)

Cry. Feel zero comfort when your youth director calls with the good news that the church wants to buy a hundred jars of cookie butter to support you.

Or when your little sister proudly brings home twenty-two more T-shirt orders.

Or when your YouTube rant called "Political Correctness Ruins Every Single Good Idea" goes viral.

It's all useless. Everything you do ends up as a dramatic fail. And you're not even a dramatic person! AT ALL! It's just that you have *literally* the very worst luck in the history of teenagers.

When you tell this to your mom, she suggests that you go out for the school play and put your melodrama to good use. Tell her "Ha ha. You're not funny."

But secretly you wonder if acting might really be your THING.

6. This is your circus. These are your monkeys. You need so much help.

Spend three days in solitary silence, finding your purpose in cutting out dozens of tiny #p!nkit! T-shirts to fill the growing stack of orders.

Decide you must outsource the actual sewing to your grandma, who makes the bobbins and thread cooperate like she's been doing this for a hundred years. Technically she kind of *has* been doing this for a hundred years. This is also depressing because that means your grandma found *her* thing when she was younger than you are now.

Because you are still a kind person—despite your hardships—agree to give your little sister a free shirt for helping you sell so many.

But when she tries it on, you nearly black out with hysteria. Why does this look so weird? Why are the armholes so low? Accuse your sister of having weirdly placed arms, which begins a fight so ugly that she yells, "YOU ARE SUCH A LOSER. YOU LITERALLY RUINED YOUR ONLY PART OF THIS SHIRT BUSINESS."

She is right. You have cut the shirts *so wrong* that the only way anyone could wear one would be to hunch over like an ape.

When your sister announces you'll have to rename the shirts #Pr!matePink!, you dissolve into tears.

Cry harder when you overhear her asking Grandma if the two of them can keep the business going without you.

7. You have found your purpose. It is SO depressing. Ugh.

Decide you will just live in an old bus on the edge of town for the rest of your life because you cannot get anything right—maybe not even that. You would probably find a way to fall into the river. Or break the broken-down bus.

At least you could be an example to your friends of what not to become.

Maybe this is God's plan for your life. Maybe He will send people to see you in your junky bus as an example of what happens to those who never find their thing.

Or maybe you are supposed to be the person God put on earth so His other children can learn radical patience and kindness. You are like the difficult person Jesus had to teach other people how to love. You're Zacchaeus. But without the happy ending.

8. Life tastes delicious–like cookies and cream.

But what's this? Apparently the world has fallen in love with the crunchy-creamy goodness of OreoButter. You have orders for 102 more—even with the offensive (eye roll) name.

Have so much fun blending up thousands of Oreos with your youth squad. Snort-laugh when you tell your people the terrible story about the #Pr!matePink! shirts. Show them pictures of the fashion disasters, and howl at the sleeves that look like poorly placed pockets. Everyone decides you should start a new trend called #OddPocketP!nk!

These are your people. They get you.

Donate $600 more to the nursing home so they can buy a popcorn machine for their media room. Nothing can discourage you, even when the Facebook trolls point out that old people can't really eat popcorn, because, dentures.

Rise above the temptation to argue THAT REALLY IS AGEISM. Pray for these mean internet people who obviously need a Savior so badly.

9. Become the misunderstood hometown hero.

Well, look at that. As it turns out, becoming a YouTube sensation really did turn out to be your thing. When the Hometown Heroes segment on the local news mentions your cookie butter nonprofit and vlog, you get 143 new subscribers. Your daily commentary about your own life goes viral.

Scroll through your old videos, proud of every important vlog you've done this year. Beam at yourself as you deliver important journalism about the medical dangers of basketball—complete with a selfie of you playing in that football helmet.

Rewatch your investigative journalism about swimming pools needing flashing lights that will alert racers of the approaching edge. This is good stuff—actual hard-hitting reporting. You are, truly, a Hometown Hero.

But wait. Most of the new comments on your vlog channel are "LOL" and that emoji that's laughing so hard it's crying.

This is an odd way to respond to critical news segments, like your tutorial on How to Fix a Fashion Mistake by Adding Extra Sleeves.

Wait. Do all these people think your vlog is supposed to be funny? Oh, wow. That's so offensive. And embarrassing.

This is why the internet is stupid and needs to be shut down.

10. You are a person who needs God to use His loud voice.

Decide that you actually know zero percent of anything at all.

Seriously. Your dog has more talent in his little toenail than you do. Announce to God that you are OFFICIALLY done trying to find your thing. You are now just relying on Him every second of every day to show you what to do next. You cannot be trusted in any sport, business, charity, or fashion endeavor.

You are only allowed to serve in the ways that He clearly sends you. Currently that only seems to include making (eating) lots of cookie butter. You can do that. You are a faithful person who is patient—and now a little addicted to pulverized cookies.

(*But a LOUD voice would be especially appreciated here, God. Because anything else will absolutely turn out to be a disaster.* You pray for God to YELL what He wants you to do next. Because #confused.)

11. God hears you. You hear God. This is not subtle AT ALL.

Oh, that's super funny, God. Ha ha. A hearing aid drive BECAUSE YOU ARE SO SUBTLE, LORD.

Okay, yes, you will HEAR Him on this one and make enough OreoButter for Old-Timers that you can buy hearing-aid batteries for the whole nursing home.

Plus, yes, the basketball team needs an announcer. When the coach tells you that everyone would love to HEAR your hilarious take on the games, you tell God you hear Him loud and clear. Nothing subtle about this.

When your little sister asks you to design earrings to match the #p!nkit! shirts, you just cannot believe that God is taking this whole HEARING thing so far.

(Pro tip: earrings are 5 BILLION times easier to make than shirts.)

GOD'S SILVER (GLITTER) LINING

By the time you're a teenager, you've heard lots of times that God has a plan for your life. Or you might have heard the cousin advice to this, adults telling their stories of how they discovered God's plan for their lives.

The story always seems to go the same. This teen was trying to discover God's specific purpose for her life, but she was on the wrong track. And then, suddenly, with a flash of lightning, she understood who God had created her to be. Finally, she became a medical missionary or cupcake baker or sand volleyball player, and she understood why God had put her on this earth. It's all good, and it's all for God.

The reality is, though, most of us don't know what we're supposed to do with our lives. We want to serve God, we want to create or do something significant, but we don't know what that looks like exactly. Where are the blueprints, God?

The Bible doesn't give us detailed plans about how to find God's plan for each of our lives. Jesus never outlines the easy three-step plan to finding your specific purpose.

But Scripture is filled with the work that God wants all of us to do. This work includes sharing His Word with the world, serving others, learning to live humbly, trusting Him, encouraging and forgiving, and sharing the light of His love with a world in darkness.

Living out your story as His daughter won't look exactly like mine, or your best friend's, or even your parents' story. Your Father has given you specific talents and experiences and passions that will make your story unique.

Trust Him to help you find your voice and your way to shine for Him with your individual light.

The world needs the beautiful light that you shine to better see the Savior who gives it to you.

CONVERSATION SPARKS

1. Talk about the talents God has given you and ones He has not. Make a list of what you really enjoy doing (sports, subjects in school, church activities, hobbies, or other experiences). Also, list activities you've tried that don't seem to be your thing at all.

2. True or false: God has given you a specific purpose for your individual life. Explain your answer.

3. Psalm 119:105 says, "Your word is a lamp to my feet and a light to my path." Talk about how the Bible can give each of us the encouragement and guidance we need to understand His plan for our lives.

SHINE ON!

Dear Father, You know me so well and understand who I am in such wonderful ways. Help me to see myself the way that You see me, Lord. Show me Your will and guide me to live it out in my life. Lead me to shine Your light to the world, who needs Jesus. In Your name. Amen.

(Fake) Frequently Asked Questions about Serving

Question 1

My favorite part of serving is finishing. I really like posting pictures of myself building houses or helping at my church's homeless pantry. I know the pictures aren't really the point, but I can't help it. Everyone LOVES this stuff and that makes me feel good. But then I feel terrible that I'm kind of shallow about serving. Is it bad that I only want to volunteer so people think I'm a good person?

Answer

That's definitely normal. Our human hearts are tuned to hear the sound of praise—and the click of "likes" on Snapchat. No matter how good your intentions to help for the sake of serving God, pride will make you want more of the compliments and the feeling that you are a very good person.

But also trust that more is going on here than that. You're learning when you serve—about the hungry people you can help feed or why families need more stable housing. Pray for God to keep showing ways the world needs the light you can share—and not just to score more thumbs-up emojis on the pictures of you doing it.

Question 2

Define *serving*—because I am trying here, but I have literally zero time. I have soccer practice, AP classes, and an afterschool job. Plus I'm trying to take care of myself and be a good friend. Also I do go to church on Sundays, and that takes time too.

When am I *seriously* supposed to add serving to that schedule? Midnight? Get up at 4 a.m.?

Answer

Okay, so let's talk about vocation. Vocation is the idea that you're called to serve in all these roles where God has already put you. Soccer player. Student. Friend. Daughter. You can serve here. You probably already are.

Because service is much more about a change of attitude than a different atmosphere. It's bringing the love of Christ wherever you go. It's putting others first, modeling what it means to trust in your Savior.

When Jesus defined our roles as Christians, He told us to love God and love others (Mark 12:30–31). Jesus told us to live with humility as we share the Gospel, pray, worship, and show others the kindness that God has shown us.

You can do this anywhere and all the time. This is the change of heart Jesus was talking about when He said to love God first and then love others. You don't need to slot extra time in your day to show up for that.

~~~~~~~~~~~~~

Question 3

Does anyone else think serving is kind of awkward? It's asking people to give you money. ("Here is some watery lemonade; give me a dollar for it.") Or it's so condescending. ("Homeless person, I'm sorry your life is like this. Here is a bar of soap." Because, why? They smell? That's so insulting, and I refuse to offend anyone.)

Isn't it kinder to do my own thing than accidentally insult or overcharge someone?

Answer

Part of serving is getting out of your comfort zone and connecting with people. Here's the deal. Looking into the eyes of someone who hasn't eaten in a couple of days can feel awkward. You might feel ashamed for all the blessings you have. Or you might feel ashamed for them.

Say the truest, kindest thing you can to this person. Pray for this person, who is God's child, someone Jesus died on the cross to save. And if he (or she) is open to it, offer to grab his hands and pray with him. Or just listen. Be patient here. Ask yourself, "What might God's love feel like for this person in this moment?"

So, yes. Serving is a little awkward. But that's part of how the process of putting others first changes you—and blesses those you are serving.

~~~~~~~~~~

Question 4

Some of these mission trips and service ideas don't feel very safe. I heard about these people who went to Haiti and crashed their bus. And my sister's friend's cousin was cyberstalked when she was crowdfunding money for her mission trip. Most service projects are too dangerous. Does God really want us to put ourselves in these scary situations? I don't think so!

Answer

Sometimes the excuses can fill up our minds so there is no room for just doing the work. This is exactly what Satan and the most selfish parts of our hearts want to happen. When we imagine all the reasons that serving is a bad idea, we stay in our comfortable houses, not doing the work that might help others and point them to Jesus.

Obviously, be safe. Use common sense, and never put yourself in a truly dangerous situation.

But also don't let fear keep you from being the hands and feet of Jesus to those who need it most.

~~~~~~~~~~

Question 5

To be honest, I really don't think any of these people deserve all this serving. Our youth group was supposed to cut all these fancy crafts for the Sunday School kids. Seriously? No one did that for us. Also, I've heard that these "economically disadvantaged" people are really not so bad off. They just want the free food.

Even worse, I heard that some people in other countries get better clothes than we do. And someone posted about these kids who got iPads for Christmas. They came with the Bible preloaded on them. Do you think the kids read the Bible when they could be playing games? Probably not.

Answer

Yep, probably some of this is true. But there are some parts of life that you absolutely cannot judge, measure, or predict. Hospitality, love, and grace fall into the "unmeasurable" category.

Are some people in the world of charity corrupt? Of course. Corruption is as old as the human heart. Do some people take advantage of others? Every millisecond of every day.

But this is, perhaps, one of the greatest blessings of learning to serve. When you have faith that you are shining God's love, it lets you trust that you have nothing to lose.

In other words, you get over yourself and start seeing yourself as a helper instead of a victim. This is what happens when you share grace or show hospitality.

You are reflecting God's love, and that means you are making the right difference. Trust Him for the details.

~~~~~~~~~~

Question 6

Not to be rude, but telling other people to believe in Jesus feels forced and not very effective. I feel like some Bible beater, or worse, one of those people who stands on the corner telling everyone that they had better love God or else they'll go to hell.

That's the picture I imagine when I think of someone telling other people about God. And I honestly don't think that's me. Sorry.

Answer

It's the rare person who can share the Gospel with a megaphone and an actual soapbox.

You've probably already figured out that most people aren't walking around actively worrying about what might happen to their soul for eternity. However, most people are worried about something very real.

Some people need a home that keeps out the rain. Or some people are thirsty. Or hungry. Some moms are frantic about not having Christmas gifts to give their families. Many people are fighting a hard battle with a chronic disease or a tough relationship, or they are very lonely.

When Jesus tells us to be the light of the world, He is talking about doing good works that point to our Lord in heaven. This is showing the lonely, the poor, the hungry, and the sad the Good News about their Savior.

Jesus gives us an action plan for this. He tells us in Matthew 25:31–46 to feed the hungry, clothe the homeless, and give water to thirsty people. This gives hope to God's people in ways they understand right now.

GOD'S SILVER (GLITTER) LINING

You're a smart girl, and you've probably already learned the answers to most of these questions. Your generation is constantly learning ways to show God's love. More than ever before, teens are aware of global poverty and how Christians can show God's love to those who are living in darkness.

This is an exciting time for you, as you find new ways to serve around the world and also in your very own communities. Our family is working alongside teenagers who are fighting against sex trafficking, who are packing Christmas gifts and shipping them off to other countries, who travel all over the United States to build homes, and who serve right in their own backyard.

Here's my favorite story of the last kind of serving:

Our church is in the old-town part of our city. Every year the city puts on a Rice Harvest Festival. But somehow, they always forget that if thousands of people are coming to a festival, it would be a good idea to provide a lot of porta potties.

Let's just say the bathroom situation at the festival is pretty stinky.

So our church opened up its doors to the steady stream of families who are crossing their legs. Our youth group provides air conditioning and seats, a place for moms to breastfeed or for kids to take a break from walking.

Volunteers keep the bathrooms stocked and play with kids who are tired of the dizzying carnival rides outside.

We also have prayer teams on hand in case someone has a spiritual need (in addition to the obvious physical one of having to pee). We share information about Jesus, our congregation, and the preschool. We give out free Bibles, and our pastor is there for anyone who has questions.

This is kindness. It's meeting an urgent physical need of a whole bunch of people.

Every year when our family shows up to help at the festival, I'm reminded of how simple serving God can be.

The message that God will take care of you, that He loves you, and that Jesus died for your sins really is the best news. People need this love. Many of them will come into our church to fill their water bottles at the water fountain—but they will leave with so much more. Prayer. God's Word. Answers to their questions. The love of their Savior.

This is what it looks like to shine God's love to those who need it.

CONVERSATION SPARKS

1. Talk about the reasons most people hesitate to serve. Are many of us scared? unsure where to start? afraid we'll get it wrong? Or are our reasons deeper–selfishness, laziness, or pride? What help does God give us to equip us to serve?

2. Read Matthew 5:16. What are the "good works" that give glory to our Father in heaven?

3. Write a prayer asking God to help you better understand service as a vocation and how He wants you to help further His kingdom of believers.

SHINE ON!

Dear Jesus, thank You for Your perfect example of service. Thank You for loving people well by feeding them and caring for them, and for dying on the cross for all of us. Help me to follow Your example of perfect humility and love. In Your holy name. Amen.

Show Up!

(Seven Ways to Serve by Showing Up)

Take the fancy mission trips that require a passport. Definitely do all of those car washes with epic water fights. Help run the PowerPoint at church every Sunday or play your trumpet in the Easter service.

Absolutely yes to baking chocolate chip cookies for that bake sale, and for sure help at the pancake breakfast, where you serve hundreds of thick, syrup-covered pancakes as big as your face.

Yes to all of this.

But also, yes to another kind of serving, the kind Jesus did all through the Bible.

Yes to the Ministry of Showing Up.

1. When a friend is hurting after a breakup . . . show up.

If this has been you—if you've gone through a hard breakup—you know how powerful and healing it is to have your people around you. You feel loved when real people show up with hugs and laughter and conversation and care.

Yes, many of them will text or reach out on social media, but the Ministry of Showing Up is what will let you see the love of Christ.

2. When you aren't sure what to do . . . show up.

You just heard that the new girl who sits at your lunch table got a bad diagnosis. Show up, sit next to her, and ask how she's doing. Yes, it's awkward. Sure, she might assume you're trying to get some gossip. She might give you the side-eye for only talking to her after she's got some bad drama happening in her life.

Get over the fear of that and show up anyway. Pray before you talk to her and then again after you talk to her.

Pray for Jesus to be with her through this hard time. Ask Him to help you share the right words. Tell God that you're not sure what she needs but He knows, and then ask Him to give it to her.

Trust this: your prayers and your love will last a lot longer than the awkwardness.

3. When you need to get out of your own head . . . show up.

When you feel like you are at the absolute end of yourself, like you cannot stand your own worries and judgment anymore, show up for someone else. When you're feeling sorry for yourself about your bad grades or your birthday that no one seemed to care about, show up for someone else.

This will not be what you want to do. Your own ego will tell you that you are a victim and deserve a pity party for yourself. You will feel like everyone else in the world should be helping you—not the other way around.

But this is when it's very important to get out of your own spiral. Connect with this other soul, another person who is going through a bad breakup or bad news or a bad time in her family.

Sharing God's love is exactly what this other person needs—and it's what you need too. Because, as it turns out, God's love is like actual glitter in the way that it gets all over everything. When you're showing up for this other person, God is changing your own loneliness. Through your connection with this other soul, you are hearing the Good News too, and He's helping you out of your own isolation and the craziness of your own thoughts.

This is the way God's system works. Shine the love of your Savior to someone else, and you end up brightening your own world too.

4. When there's a tragedy . . . show up.

When it comes to serving, donating money is always helpful.

But do you know what means so much more? You showing up with your arms to hug . . . your legs to do the hard work . . . and your words to encourage.

People need the Holy Spirit and the Word of God and a demonstration of what Jesus' love looks like in action. Show up with the fruit of the Spirit: love, joy, peace, patience, kindness, goodness, faithfulness, gentleness, and self-control. Be patient through their grief. Pray with the hurting. Be kind with gifts and help.

Bring the hurting what they really need—your physical body ready to work and your spirit ready to shine God's love.

5. When it's awkward . . . show up.

Most of us do whatever we can to avoid awkwardness.

It can feel like literal pain to show up at the house of your ex-best friend when you hear that her sweet grandma just died. You don't want to go in because you know it will be so incredibly awkward to see her mom, who is still mad at you. You could come up with a million excuses not to knock on that door.

But you go anyway. And it's okay. And when you hug your ex-best friend's mom and tell her how sorry you are that her mom died, she hugs you so hard that you just know this was the right thing to do.

Sometimes it seems like God is closer in awkward moments. In our vulnerability, He is right there. Connection feels different when everyone is defenseless and open and needy for God's love.

Show up—even when it's awkward—and experience a different kind of ministry, right there in the middle of this exposed, real life.

6. When it's for Jesus . . . show up.

Jesus said, "I was hungry, and you gave Me something to eat. I was thirsty, and you gave Me something to drink. I was naked, and you clothed Me. Because when you did this for the least of anyone, you did it for Me." (See Matthew 25:31–46.)

Same for showing up. When you sit with the lonely and when you include the isolated and when you visit the forgotten, you are the hands and feet of Jesus. Yes, that is an overused cliché, but it's also the truth.

7. When there are a million excuses NOT to ... show up.

Some of these excuses will sound very wise. ("It's weird to hug him." "It would be better to just leave it alone." "That might not be safe." "I think there might be a better use of my time." "I would go over there, but my week is so busy.")

Yes, of course, you should use common sense and not put yourself in any kind of danger. But most of the time, all these are just very, very good strategies to keep you comfortable and safe. You probably don't want to show up because you're avoiding the awkwardness of not knowing exactly what to say.

The truth is, you will be fine.

GOD'S SILVER (GLITTER) LINING

One of the best examples of the Ministry of Showing Up is John 11:17–44, when Lazarus dies and everyone shows up for his sisters Mary and Martha. Throughout the story, we see how the community comforts them at this really hard time (vv. 19, 33–36).

This is also the chapter of the Bible with the memorable shortest verse: "Jesus wept" (v. 35). Perhaps we can learn everything we need to know about showing up from this verse, from only two words.

What did Jesus do when His friends were hurting and His other friend was dead? He showed up, and He also showed His own tenderness and vulnerability and sadness. When Jesus saw Mary sobbing and those who loved Mary and Martha also crying, He "was deeply moved in His spirit" (v. 33) to weep with them.

Could it be considered awkward that Jesus, the one with all the answers, was crying? Sure. But Jesus still cried. He still showed real compassion, true vulnerability, and an openness to really be with those He loved.

There are so many good examples here for us: how Jesus changed His travel plans to show up for Mary and Martha; the way

He showed up completely, with an open heart and the Holy Spirit; and the kindness He showed the people He loved.

Of course, because Jesus was also true God, He performed the really important miracle of raising Lazarus from the dead. This was also showing up and serving. Jesus helped His friends by doing what only He could do.

You might not be able to fix other people's problems. But you can serve by showing up, open and vulnerable and full of love. You can share kindness and God's love and the Holy Spirit with those who need it.

You can show up, full of the light of God's love, and reflect it to those who are sitting in darkness.

CONVERSATION SPARKS

1. Talk about times you've struggled or failed to show up. Maybe you were too young or too scared or too awkward to care for someone. What did you learn from those situations? What can you pray about future opportunities that you will have to show up?

2. When Jesus came to earth as true man and true God, He showed humans what perfect comfort, perfect love, and perfect service look like. Think about Jesus' life and how He treated His friends. How would you describe this to someone who had never heard of Jesus?

3. Talk about how your church shows up for people. Think about the ministries in your congregation. How do they care for the community, and for one another, by showing up?

SHINE ON!

Dear Jesus, thank You for showing up in the most meaningful way, when You died on the cross for our sins. Help me to show up in the moments when it's hard, Lord. Give me faith to see the ways that You are sharing Your love, and give me the courage to reflect it to the world, Jesus. In Your name. Amen.

Stars in Your Eyes and Jesus in Your Heart

This is the message we have heard from Him and proclaim to you, that God is light, and in Him is no darkness at all. If we say we have fellowship with Him while we walk in darkness, we lie and do not practice the truth. But if we walk in the light, as He is in the light, we have fellowship with one another, and the blood of Jesus His Son cleanses us from all sin. If we say we have no sin, we deceive ourselves, and the truth is not in us. If we confess our sins, He is faithful and just to forgive us our sins and to cleanse us from all unrighteousness. If we say we have not sinned, we make Him a liar, and His word is not in us.

—1 JOHN 1:5–10

Here's a spoiler alert about the rest of your life: you have to learn how to forgive, and it will probably be your very hardest lesson.

People are pretty much programmed to hold grudges, to be self-righteous about wrongs against us, and to punish those who hurt us. This is our autopilot, our default tactics in relationships.

You'll feel these relationship instincts over and over, pretty much every day of your life. Your siblings will kick you or steal—and stain—your favorite sweatshirt. Bad friends will share your biggest secrets with the world. Your best friends will be just terrible at returning your texts—especially when you really need their help. Not to mention the bullies who will tease you constantly, the social media savages who will leave mean comments on your posts, and the boyfriend who will cheat on you.

The fights and abuse of a normal day are enough that you will sometimes feel like the best strategy is to live an isolated life, where you don't have to deal with people at all. In fact, many of us do decide to live exactly like this.

But that's totally ignoring the message of our whole faith. Because Jesus died on the cross to forgive our sins, we can forgive other people, and so we can be forgiven by other people.

In 1 John 1, the disciple describes this kind of life as walking in the darkness. God has given us His light through Jesus. If we refuse to forgive, we ignore His grace and live in that dark bitterness.

The light from God is the good news that we can—and should—forgive everyone. Walking in fellowship with others means giving grace to your mom when she's grouchy and snaps at you for chewing too loudly. Walking in fellowship is asking for forgiveness when you've hurt someone. It means forgiving your friends when they let you down.

Let's look at how we can shine this light of forgiveness to everyone we meet. Let's ask God to keep igniting His light so we can share the brilliant, starry-bright love with the world.

Ten Not-So-Easy Steps to Getting Along with Your Siblings

〜〜〜〜〜

1. Another day, another epic fight with your little sister.

Lose your temper like an actual professional wrestler when she (again!) steals your best silver earrings—and then loses one. Throw a chair like you are in a bad play about melodramatic rage.

Only your rage is real.

Especially when she lies to your parents and tells them that you are a crazy person who doesn't even own silver earrings and who has a compulsive lying problem. As your parents are looking at you with pity—already writing you off as the Problem Child—your horrible sister winks at you.

Scream.

Confirm parents' worst suspicions about your mental state.

2. Stop speaking to your sister completely.

Make your older brother deliver your messages to her. He is terrible at this. When you tell him, "Please ask our sister to give me back my phone charger," he forgets to. When you repeat this three more times, your brother loses his hearing.

Then your phone dies, and your sister laughs so hard she probably wets her pants. (At least you hope she does.)

Realize the hard truth that God has accidentally placed you into a family of mean idiots who have been put on this earth to terrorize you and take your things.

3. Your sister is a thief, liar, and cheater. You also feel sorry for her.

Walk into your sister's room to find your lost Converse and discover her sobbing on her bed. She is in big trouble for cheating on a test and is terrified of her punishment. Feel the tiniest trickle of compassion for this little girl (who, yes, is *still* a thief and a liar, and now also a cheater).

But you also kind of feel sorry for her.

You do love her—especially when she looks so pathetic, with her face a hot mess of snot and tears. Sit on her bed. Rub her back. Tell her that Mom and Dad won't be that hard on her because she is their favorite. Try not to dwell on that truth too much, even though it is *so obvious* and completely annoying.

Focus on the compassion you feel for her and ignore her other annoying qualities.

Hug her—and mean it . . . 97 percent.

4. And sometimes you love her so much.

No one is more surprised than you to have a really fun week with your sister. Because even though she has the obvious addictions to lying, cheating, and stealing, she is the one person on earth who knows you completely.

Laugh together every night as you watch old home videos of you two together. Feel a rush of love as you see the screen version of you rocking her itty-bitty baby self.

Wonder at the sweetness of that tiny baby. Snuggle closer with your sister and tell her that you love her more than anything. Have a little love-fest when she says she trusts you more than anyone else in the world.

Thank God for the special gift of this crazy, adorable mini-me who wants to be just like you.

Have a sleepover in her room and promise each other you will live together when you're older. She is your person. Little sisters for the win!

5. Realize older brothers are savage.

Your older brother, however, is the opposite of your person. He is, in fact, your certified enemy. Discover that he has hacked into your phone and posted several pictures of himself with these hashtags: #MyBrotherIsMyHero #GratefulHeTalksToAnIdiotLikeMe #MyBrotherIsAStud #TextMeForHisNumber.

Also, he has been borrowing your deodorant to rub on his feet before soccer practice. He also admitted last night that he uses your toothbrush to clean the spit valve of his trumpet.

Cry and moan to your parents about this savage beast who is living in your house.

Discover they actually love him better when they tell you that you're overreacting. When you try to hack into his phone for a little revenge texting, you get caught and grounded for a week.

Use this time alone in your room to plot his demise like an actual crazy person.

6. Discover the (literal) pain of little sisters.

The only person overjoyed about your grounding is your little sister. She uses the time to practically move into your room. As an annoying bonus, she talks constantly.

When you (politely!) explain that you need a tiny break from her monologue about everything wrong with seventh grade, she freaks out and slams your bedroom door.

Unfortunately, your hand was on that doorjamb. Howl in pain as she glares at you and tells you that you deserve to be hurt because you cause so much pain for everyone else.

Lose it and cry for real.

Sob about all of the injustice in your own life—your bruised hand, your abusive siblings, and your cruel parents. Fall asleep from the exhaustion of crying so hard.

Wake up to discover your mom rubbing your back and telling you that both your siblings are in big trouble for their antics. Feel a tiny bit better. Your mom cancels your grounding punishment two days early—and you feel like you might actually survive this crazy family.

7. Become a relationship expert.

Discover an apology note from your brother that is about 27 percent sincere. When you see it's signed with "I love you," you feel so touched, you decide to forgive him instantly.

Write him back a note that tells him that you're glad he is your brother. Feel very much like an expert in relationships. Consider writing a daily blog about forgiveness and how to survive very difficult family situations. Then remember that you probably won't feel this wise or loving toward your siblings tomorrow.

Give up the blog idea, but ask God to keep reminding you about forgiveness when you feel like you might be secretly adopted.

8. The family that camps together, laughs together.

Go on a weekend camping trip with your family and have the very best time in the back seat with your siblings. You dress up your ancient cocker spaniel in hats and sunglasses and post the pictures as @HankTheHipster.

Scream with laughter as the three of you create more and more ridiculous posts from your poor dog. #HankTheLactoseIntolerantBeast #HankTheSmoothJazzLover #HankTheSnowflakeIsTriggeredByYourDogWhistle

Consider that you are your funniest when you're with your brother and sister. When you catch your mom smiling at you in the rearview mirror, wink at her.

She knows you actually do adore these two goofy people.

9. Except your family is terrible.

Try REALLY hard to remember that you love your brother and sister when they constantly tease you—about how you can't throw a Frisbee; the way your breath smells in the morning; that you still sleep with your favorite stuffed kitten, Kitty Perry; and the number of times you get lost while hiking.

Have a tiny temper tantrum when it is DAY THREE OF THIS TERRIBLE TRIP and your annoying little sister and bully older brother have ganged up on you.

Inform your parents that you do NOT LIKE OR ENJOY these two creatures, even a little bit. When your mom tells you that you're just tired, lock yourself in the camper and zone out on your phone for three hours.

When your battery dies, search everywhere for your charger—only to find it in your brother's duffel bag of crusty, dirty clothes.

Wish you had the keys to the camper so you could drive home and leave them all in the woods.

10. Try to love them better.

Survive the family trip and ride home sunburned, exhausted, but sort of happy. Camping really was kind of fun, especially roasting marshmallows with your goofy little sister and the diving contest with your funny older brother. They really were sweet to help you deal with Mom and Dad's rage when you accidentally lost the only lantern.

Watch your siblings nap and decide that they are not perfect (not even like 1 percent perfect), or even that nice, but that you do love them. Deep down, you don't know what you would do without these two.

Ask God to help you love these crazy people a little better. Try a little harder to forgive—even when they "forget" to help clean out the car and you're stuck with the whole job.

GOD'S SILVER (GLITTER) LINING

If you feel like your family is *extra*, as in extra-annoying, extra-difficult, extra-selfish, extra-lovable, extra-crazy, and extra-wonderful, then you are not alone. Actually, they probably feel the same about you.

Because this is the deal with families: love them or try to leave them, they are so much a part of you. First, they are the ones who have truly known you for every bit of your life. Second, they love you unconditionally, differently than anyone else. And finally, they are the people who can be the absolute cruelest to you.

But your family is your assignment from God. These really are your people—the ones He gave you to love and care for you, to teach you, to punish you and forgive you, and to keep you on-track. But because you live so up close with your family, they also feel like the most suffocating people on earth.

Jesus was 100 percent God (perfect) but also 100 percent man (with a real flesh-and-blood family). So He knew what He was talking about when He told us how to deal with our brothers and sisters. His message was that living together with family means lots and lots of forgiveness. Yes, you will all mess up and want to disown one another many times in a week, but family is the first and the best place to learn forgiveness.

Decide you will forgive your family throughout your life—and ask God to help you with this. Understand that these are your people in so many ways, and honor that relationship by giving them grace upon grace. Tell them how you feel and forgive them quickly when they apologize.

Above all, go back to your heavenly Father, over and over, to be filled up with His light of forgiveness so you can shine it to your family.

CONVERSATION SPARKS

1. Tell a story of the hardest time you've had forgiving your family. How were you able to do this?

2. Look at Matthew 18:21-22. What does Jesus say about forgiving your brother? What point is He making here?

3. What would you tell someone who has lived through terrible sin in her family? Where can those who have been abused by family members go for help? Can they ever forgive the people who did this? How?

SHINE ON!

Lord, thank You for my family. You have given me the exact people I need, and I trust in Your perfect plan. Help me to live as Your daughter, who loves and forgives my parents and siblings. Let me shine Your light to my family. In Jesus' name. Amen.

Eight (Fake) Bible Verses about Forgiveness You Won't Find in the Bible

1. Forgive everyone, all the time—except for really annoying people and except when it's not convenient for you.

God never says, "You don't have to forgive those who bug you. Keep hating anyone with a different opinion than you."

He never says, "If someone really did something awful to you, it's on them. You can silently judge them for being terrible. Never forget that you are the best and they are terrible sinners."

Instead, we are all filled up with sin and need God's grace. Spread it around to everyone—even those people who annoy and inconvenience you.

2. Your forgiveness is a precious gift that you must savor and save.

The good news here is that Jesus never taught, "I'm giving you only a tiny bit of forgiveness. Watch how you use this. You can't spend too much of it in one place. Forgive only those who are very worthy of it, and do it only on extremely special occasions. But whatever you do, don't run out of forgiveness, because you don't have much of it!"

Totally the opposite, actually. Forgiveness is bottomless, endless, without boundaries. You can't run out of it, ever.

3. Forgiving your enemies is the easiest part of your day.

Good news! Forgiving other people is mindless, right up there with online shopping and eating chocolate. Giving grace to people who have hurt you is SO easy!

Hmm. God doesn't say this because it's not true. If you've ever forgiven someone, you know that it's pretty much exactly opposite of what your heart wants to do.

4. You will be forgiven for a few of your sins. Not the really big ones. Not the ones you're most ashamed of. Definitely not the sins God is mad at you about.

For some reason, this is a weird belief we all carry around. It's not true, though.

It's actually so completely untrue. God is all about total forgiveness, all the time. His mercy covers your big sins, your small sins, and even the ones you keep replaying in your head because you're so ashamed of them.

All of them—gone. Wiped clean. Totally.

5. The world will know you are Christians by your excellent ability to judge, to hate, to point out people's flaws, and to hold on to bitterness.

If another girl spreads gossip about you, show her that you are a Christian by spreading gossip about her. If a boy embarrassed you on the first day of middle school, really hate him forever and ever. Don't let one day slip by where you forget to hate him.

Be tenacious about holding on to any wrongs done to you. This will show everyone what a Christian really looks like.

Oh, wait. None of this is true. Fruit of the Spirit, not fruit of the flesh (which would be hating, bitterness, and meanness).

6. Keep a record of wrongs against you.

Ahhh. This is exactly what we all want to believe. When your enemies get to ten sins, you don't have to forgive them anymore. There is a maximum amount of sins, and it's your job to keep track of who has offended and hurt you.

Be sure to count all those sins so you'll know when anyone has crossed The Line of Unforgiveness. Maybe write down the sins against you, if that helps. Otherwise just hold them in your heart.

Except, just kidding. Don't do any of this. That's a terrible way to live, and God is very clear about that in the Bible.

7. God hates all the same people you do.

You don't even have to bother with anyone who annoys you, because they're a lost cause. The homeless people who beg instead of getting a job? God probably thinks they're lazy and don't even deserve a job. That's what you think, so it's probably what He does too.

The girls in your school who have sex, get pregnant, and then get abortions? God is so done with them. He knows they're not even worth His time. He probably can't forgive them either.

The criminals? God thinks all the same things about them that you do—worthless, too hard-hearted, never going to get out of their sin.

Only this isn't how God feels at all. In fact, if you feel like God hates all the same people you do, you might have created God in your own image.

8. You are so good that you don't need any forgiveness.

Congratulations to you, Christian Girl. Because you are so dedicated to going to church, wearing Christian T-shirts, telling everyone about your good habits, and posting Bible verses, you don't even need forgiveness.

All this religious stuff you do makes you absolutely perfect. Just a couple of things to work on, and you're right there at the top of heaven, Jesus status almost.

It's your good works that earn God's grace. If you'll spend enough time kneeling on the hard floor or serving the poor, He will be so impressed, He will let you into heaven.

LOL. Not really at all. We all need God's grace all the time. Sorry.

GOD'S SILVER (GLITTER) LINING

These fake Bible verses are silly, sarcastic—and also totally what we believe sometimes.

We convince ourselves that some people just aren't worthy of our forgiveness. Or—and this is a crowd favorite—we believe grace is very limited, like money in a bank account. If you spend too much in one place, it will run out. And then sometimes we believe that we are so moral, we don't really need a Savior; we just need to try harder to be good.

You're old enough now to understand that none of this is really true. Instead, the truth is this: because Jesus lived a perfect life, then died for our sins, God forgives every one of us forever and ever. This also means that you can forgive everyone who hurts you, and everyone can forgive you for your mistakes. God's grace never runs out. This is such a better system than the one we would create.

Also, this message is why the Bible is so radical and its story of grace is so exciting—because this is true love.

And so, you beautiful, light-filled girl, what does it mean to shine this love to the world? It means sharing God's message of perfect grace with everyone.

Share it by trusting that God has enough grace to keep forgiving you.

Shine it by showing the world His unconditional love—even for people you don't agree with (or even really like at first).

Shine it by forgiving all the people, all the time. Trust that your Creator and Redeemer wants you to spread around forgiveness like sparkly silver glitter.

CONVERSATION SPARKS

1. True or false: God's grace feels unnatural to us. Why or why not?

2. Look at Matthew 18:15–20; Luke 6:37; and Matthew 5:23–24. What does Jesus teach about forgiveness?

3. Choose your favorite forgiveness Bible verse (one that really is in the Bible) and talk about what it means to you. Memorize the verse and journal about how this verse becomes more meaningful in your faith story as you put it into practice.

SHINE ON!

O Lord, thank You for Your Word and for Your forgiveness. As I learn more about Your grace, I'm amazed by Your mercy, Father. Let me love Your people better, dear Lord, by forgiving them often and by shining Your grace to the world. In Jesus' name. Amen.

Pinterest Fails
and Internet Forgiveness

Like most disappointing, crazy ideas, this one started with a picture I found on the internet. It was a craft idea from Pinterest, and it looked so easy and cute that it seemed too good to be true. (Spoiler alert: it totally was.)

I should have known better about Pinterest ideas. Our family had already had our share of #Pinterestfails. We had attempted cathedral cakes that looked like outhouses. We'd stirred up gallons of slime that remained gloopy, gluey messes. There was also the experiment with making our own bath bombs that left so much essential oil in the water we looked like seals that had survived an oil slick. We've made Christmas T-shirts with poorly placed (a-*hem*) jingle bells and no-bake cookies that easily could have been used for baseballs (except they were harder).

But my worst Pinterest fail was one that began with the best intentions. When my novel *Last Summer at Eden* came out a couple of years ago, I was so excited to share the camp love with the world, so I decided to send out Counselor Care Packages.

I searched the internet for The Best Care Packages for Camp Counselors. Among the hundreds of cute projects was the best idea: make chocolate chip cookies and ship them in upcycled Pringles containers. You could also decorate the cookie tube with construction paper and stickers. Your favorite counselor (or camper) would have a full belly and full heart because of your clever care package. Plus—bonus!—no crumbled cookies, thanks to this clever mailing tube.

Because I can be a person of extremes, I didn't want to mail cookies to only a few counselors. I wanted this to be an EPIC GIVEAWAY. I would make it a whole Instagram contest, complete with hundreds and hundreds of cookies, dozens of adorable packages, and all the #lastsummerateden love.

But first, Pringles. I needed to find potato crisps—*cheap*—so I could reuse their packages. I checked all the local grocery stores, went to Costco, and even searched for generic Pringles that might have the same tube packaging. But it turns out that Pringles are expensive—especially when you need about fifty packages.

At this point, I should have seen that the Pringles weren't really fulfilling the upcycled purpose of the craft. It wasn't like I just had dozens of cans lying around that I needed to use up. Buying all those chips would be expensive, and I wouldn't be able to send out very many packages.

Enter online shopping. Not Amazon—because that was still pricey—but a random online grocer who had cases of Pringles for cheap! cheap! cheap! Yes, the website was a bit odd, but these chips were so discounted that I didn't care.

I announced the contest on social media, and my daughters, Catie and Elisabeth, went to work baking hundreds of perfectly crispy chocolate chip cookies. I mean they baked like it was their J-O-B. Which, I suppose, it was, since I paid them in chocolate.

When the Pringles shipment arrived, I tore it open, only to discover fifty MINI Pringles tubes. They were tiny—half the size of what I was hoping.

I checked the website, and the picture was definitely of a full-size container. I emailed the company about the mix-up. I expected them to respond with "Oh, wow. LOL. We are so sorry. You're right. We accidentally sent some weird, tiny cans. Your correct order will be there ASAP."

Except that didn't happen. Instead, there was no response. Not even a "we got your message and are looking into it" kind of answer. Pound for pound, these chips were more expensive than steak. And I wasn't any closer to my goal of counselor care packages. I was starting to realize that I had been scammed.

Meanwhile, because social media stops for no one, I had families from all over the country nominating counselors to be among the lucky winners of the cute care packages.

What a disaster.

The worst part was my anger about it all. Because I felt like an idiot. This was all supposed to be a Random Act of Kindness . . . a surprise treat for counselors who were spending their summer in the sun, telling kids about Jesus. And I was messing it up. I wouldn't be able to send out wonderful packages—these would be weird and small and nothing like I was promoting on Instagram.

I planned the snarkiest of snarky reviews about that online grocery store. If the keyboard is mightier than the sword, I was about to cut them to ribbons for their terrible customer service. Because, did I mention that the horrible-no-good-online grocery store had a strict NO RETURNS policy? And they still weren't answering my emails?

Then, the whole situation got worse. My husband opened one of the Pringles cans and discovered shards of chips inside. Not just a few broken ones, like you might expect from the WORST COMPANY IN THE WORLD, but potato-crisp fragments. Practically potato dust. Oh, just wonderful. I had ordered from the only online store that uses angry, clumsy bears to package their products.

Back to the email, back to the phone, back to trying to let this company know that they could not, would not treat their customers like this. I felt cheated, and that felt bad. My bitterness at myself and at this terrible company was eating me up.

Then, somehow, it all changed. It started with me eating my first can of Pringles and realizing the age-old truth that fried potatoes with lots of salt are always really delicious.

Next, a friend had the perfect recipe for Potato Chip Fried Chicken, and it included the step of having to crush the chips. Ha. Just kidding. No, you don't. Here are enough crushed chips to batter up every chicken in Texas. Our family loved this recipe, and we went through another ten cans making Potato Chip Fried Chicken for our friends.

We also discovered that Pringles are SO GOOD covered in melted chocolate (because, health). They're especially good mixed with caramel and frozen into a salty, creamy, chocolate bark of pure deliciousness.

Around this same time, a friend found cheap camp-theme journals, and my publishing house sent me fun *Last Summer at Eden* posters. We decorated the empty Pringles cans with stickers and letters, and they did turn out to look like something Pinterest-worthy. A plan was coming together for the Counselor Care Package Giveaway, and it was actually pretty amazing.

It was seriously time for me to give up the bitterness about one unresponsive grocery store. So many good things were happening here: the counselors would receive fun, encouraging packages; we had blessed people with potato chip goodness; and we had all learned a valuable lesson about online shopping.

The last step was for me to forgive that company—and for me to forgive myself. I decided not to write the really nasty review and post it all over the internet. I did share my experience on Google reviews. I reported the facts, in case it could help someone else. But I left off the all-caps, crazy-person rant.

The packages went out, the fun pictures of counselors eating cookies covered Instagram, and I finished the whole escapade a little wiser about Pinterest and online shopping—and a lot wiser about what a relief it is to forgive.

This was God's plan all along, of course. He sent His Son, Jesus, to die for our sins so we could know the relief of forgiveness. And our heavenly Father keeps refreshing the forgiveness all the time—through His Word and Sacraments.

Because of God's grace, we can forgive ourselves, our neighbors, and even those we meet on the internet.

GOD'S SILVER (GLITTER) LINING

Agree or disagree: the internet brings out the ugliest hate in all of us.

Most of us agree that there's something about the vagueness of online relationships that allows people to get very judgy, very quickly.

Political "discussions" are completely different over Facebook than they are face-to-face. We feel free to criticize people—Democrats or Republicans, companies, and leaders—with a new brand of meanness. It's like we forget there are real people on the other end of the keyboard. So many of us fire critical, hurtful words at one another, without worrying about the effect.

Except internet fights are really no different from any other kind of fight. Even if you can't see the person you're hurting, you still have a responsibility to be kind. And when you are the one who has been offended on the internet, you can still forgive.

Jesus taught this over and over about real-life relationships. Don't carry your burden of anger or bitterness around. Realize that we are all so, so filled with sin, and we all need grace. We forgive because it's what others do for us—it's what God did for us.

It's like a muscle, this grace thing. The more you practice it, the easier it feels. If there is one thing—one tiny thing—that this world needs more of, it's those who are quick to forgive.

This dark world needs the sparkle of Christ followers who trust that He is taking care of us in all the important ways, and that means we can care for one another by forgiving.

CONVERSATION SPARKS

1. Tell your story of a time when someone has lied to you or cheated you. Why did you want to hold on to the bitterness against him or her? How did you forgive that person?

2. Read John 8:1-12. When the Pharisees brought the woman who had committed adultery to Jesus, He told them not to condemn her–unless they were perfect. They walked away, and the accused woman was let free and walked away too. Talk about this. What is the message of forgiveness in this story?

3. Read John 8:12 again. How does Jesus describe Himself? What does this mean for us?

SHINE ON!

Heavenly Father, thank You for sending Your Son, Jesus, to die on the cross for my sins. Your grace heals me, and Your salvation makes me Your child. Help me to trust that You truly have forgiven my sins. You help me, in turn, to forgive others who have hurt me. I want to live as Your redeemed daughter forever. In Jesus' loving name. Amen.

Seven Stories of Forgiveness

(Rated on a Five-Star Scale)

Of course you can't really rate forgiveness on a five-star scale. A five-star scale is what we use to measure how good a thing is. Forgiveness is God's grace; it is impossible to measure because it's impossible to imagine just how good it is.

But the five-star scale is a valuable tool. We speak to one another in the language of this scale. We rely on it to communicate how much we like or dislike something. ("Four stars for the delicious banana pancakes and one star for the slow service," or "This app is two stars because it's helpful but also crashes constantly.")

The five-star scale is a superconvenient way to summarize a lot of information. So let's give it a try. Here are famous forgiveness stories from the Bible and their possible ratings on a five-star scale.

FORGIVENESS STORY 1

That time Joseph saw the bigger thing God was doing (Genesis 37–50).

★★★★☆ for Joseph's forgiveness (because he can see the larger plans God has for his life, even when he could have totally acted like a victim).

★★★★★ for God's forgiveness because He redeems this dysfunctional relationship between Joseph and his brothers and makes them the structure for the twelve tribes of His people. Just, wow.

If you're ever tempted to feel like a victim (teacher doesn't like you, you're bullied by the Queen Bees, your hair has a weird curl thing that makes it look like you're trying to pull off a mullet), please consider Joseph.

He lived an entire misunderstood life with so many plot twists it makes the drama on *Riverdale* look boring. Here are a few of the injustices he endured: brothers tried to kill him, his boss's wife falsely accused him of rape, and he lived in a dungeon for many of his good years. If there's one person who could have thrown a self-pity party, it would be Joseph.

Except for two interesting parts of his story. First, he doesn't see himself as a victim; and second, God never leaves him in the well (or dungeon) of life. Joseph's heavenly Father keeps protecting and promoting him.

The story climaxes when Joseph finds himself face-to-face with his brothers, the same people who wanted him dead and who are now begging him for a handout. They are starving and scared and don't recognize him. (Is it the low blood sugar, brothers?)

Joseph has this dramatic perfect moment when he can choose to send them to the proverbial well of their own hunger forever. But he does not. Instead, he has one of those moments of spiritual clarity that must come straight from the Holy Spirit.

In Genesis 50:20, Joseph forgives his brothers and then says, "You meant evil against me, but God meant it for good."

Bam. Drop the mic, Joseph. This pretty much sums up all of what we believe as Christians. Haters are going to hate, but God is telling a better story in our lives than that.

Forgive your family and your friends—and even your enemies— because your heavenly Father has better plans for you.

FORGIVENESS STORY 2

That time when the big cheater King David had to forgive himself (2 Samuel 11–12).

★★★★☆ for David's forgiveness of himself (mostly because of
the beautiful psalm he wrote about it).

★★★★★ for God's forgiveness that is complete, even when we
have real-life consequences of our sins.

If you've ever screamed at a friend, cheated on a boyfriend, spread mean gossip, or lied to cover up a mistake, you've had to live with the consequences of your sin.

You're no longer trusted. Your words have permanently hurt someone you love. The person you betrayed is angry with you.

Yes, you are forgiven. Yes, you are sorry and trying to change. Yes, you really have moved past the painful episode. But there is still the reality of what you've created in your real life.

This happened to David when he committed some of the most notorious sins in the Bible. He had an affair with the beautiful Bathsheba, who also happened to be married. Then, to cover up his adultery, he had Bathsheba's husband killed.

Thanks to David's friend Nathan, who was a prophet from God, David realized his sins and knew God forgave him. What a perfect conclusion to this sinful season of David's life.

Except that this isn't the end of the story. Turns out, Bathsheba was pregnant with David's child. Even as the two tried to make the best of the situation, they couldn't undo the sins they'd committed. Bathsheba gave birth to the baby, and the baby died. David was left with terrible grief.

David had to grapple with the fact that he was truly forgiven in God's eyes, and he still had to deal with the earthly consequences.

David writes the beautiful Psalm 51, especially verses 10–12, about his need for forgiveness and how wonderful God is to give us this grace we need so badly.

God gave David and Bathsheba another son, Solomon, who became their adored child and eventual king.

Good job, God. Another example of how You turn our messes into new stories with Your five-star forgiveness.

FORGIVENESS STORY 3

That time hard-hearted Jonah wouldn't forgive a whole nation of people (Jonah 4:9–11).

★★☆☆☆ for Jonah's forgiveness because while he really does try, he just can't get over his terrible dislike for the Ninevites.

★★★★★ for God's forgiveness because He forgives the Ninevites and Jonah (and, well, everyone).

You know about Jonah from the story about the fish that threw him up on the beach. But you probably have more in common with this Old Testament missionary than you thought.

Here's a little backstory about why Jonah found himself in a fish's belly in the first place. God sent him to Nineveh to tell the Ninevites to repent. But Jonah decided the Ninevites were so evil that they didn't even deserve to hear that God loved them. The Ninevites were basically the terrorists of their day. Nineveh was the capital of Assyria, which was a cruel and ruthless nation bent on conquering the world. They were known for completely destroying cities, killing anyone in their way. Jonah decided they all deserved to go to hell, and so he sailed to Tarshish instead.

Savage, right?

Except not really savage at all. Jonah's reaction is exactly what we feel when we look at others and write them off as a lost cause. We point to another family, school, city, clique, country, or religion and announce, "There is no way God could love them."

We really don't get to judge, though. We don't get to "pull a Jonah" and decide that we are the spiritual authority on who gets God's love and who doesn't.

This is completely against the very idea of God, who loves everyone. He is all about second, four-hundredth, millionth chances to tell them that. He wants all His people to come to Him—even those who have left Him, who preach against Him, and who say He doesn't exist.

Jonah does eventually go to Nineveh (after a detour in the belly of the fish), and the Ninevites do repent and follow God. But Jonah just can't get over his prejudice against the Ninevites, and he pouts that now they know about God's wonderful love for them.

This feels pretty true to how we feel about God's grace for the people we don't like. Still, God keeps telling us to see ourselves as sharers of His grace and to leave the judging to Him.

FORGIVENESS STORY 4

That time the unforgiving servant wanted forgiveness—but he didn't want to give forgiveness himself (Matthew 18:21–35).

★☆☆☆☆ for the unforgiving servant.

★★★★★ for the forgiving king.

In Jesus' parable, the unforgiving servant wanted forgiveness. He had been charging up the New Testament version of a ginormous credit card debt. When the bill (with the king) came, he couldn't pay it.

He reacted like we all do when we've done something dumb: he freaked out and begged for mercy. The king felt so sorry for this servant that he forgave him the huge amount of money.

After the king canceled the debt—and the servant was out of credit jail—the servant conveniently forgot that grace ever existed.

He forgot so well that when he saw someone who owed him just a tiny bit of money, he was, like, "OH, NO YOU DON'T," and beat up the poor guy.

Yes yes, we know this kind of forgiveness because we are all so guilty of it. This is the rule of What's Fair for Me Is Not Fair for You.

We are all very good at demanding grace, but we aren't so good at making sure we give grace. This instinct is pretty much as human as craving chocolate.

And yet we have the perfect example of grace from God. Give it, accept it, and lean into the whole thing—because there is just as much nourishment in letting someone off the hook as there is in getting off the hook yourself.

FORGIVENESS STORY 5

That time the prodigal son came back, and his dad forgave him—but his brother wouldn't (Luke 15:11–32).

★★★★★ for the father's forgiveness.

★☆☆☆☆ for the older brother's forgiveness.

Jesus told another parable, and this one was about the lost son. The son demands his dad's money so he can run off and live a wild, R-rated life. He trashes his family's name and feels bad about it only after he has lost everything and is hungry and homeless.

When he comes back home, full of regret, his dad forgives him and throws him a big welcome-home party.

The father's forgiveness in this story is Jesus' example of how God forgives each of us. It's five-star forgiveness because it's perfect.

But the older brother struggles to forgive. When he sees his little brother coming home, he doesn't think, "Aw, this is great for everyone! My brother gets to be part of the family again. Let's get this party started!"

Instead, the big brother is all bitterness. His heart is not only three sizes too small, but he is also sneering and whining instead of joining the party.

Maybe you've been there too. Someone messes up, and part of you is giddy because now you get to be the good one. You have never looked better than when you're standing next to the Original Benedict Arnold.

But Jesus' point was for us to join the party. Quit keeping score, go enjoy the free grace, and celebrate that it belongs to all of us.

FORGIVENESS STORY 6

That time Peter pulled a total jerk move and pretended he didn't know Jesus (Matthew 26:30–35, 69–75; John 21:15–17).

★★★★★ for the forgiveness that Jesus shows.

★★★★☆ for Peter because he does mess up, but he accepts Jesus' forgiveness.

Oh, Peter. In your most famous moments, you are still kind of a hot mess. ("I want to walk on water. Ack! HELP! I can't walk on water." . . . "Hey Jesus, who is Your BEST friend, like Your *very favorite* disciple?" . . . "Oh, really? You want a piece of me? Because I will take a piece of YOUR EAR!")

Just a few hours after Peter had sliced off the high priest's servant's ear for daring to mess with Jesus, Peter used his same passion to declare that he didn't even know Jesus.

This is one of those sins with so many levels in the story. First, Jesus told Peter that he would do this exact jerk move, and Peter was outraged and insisted that he would never abandon his Savior. He promised that he would always stick up for Jesus against the political pressure of any government.

Oops. Except if they're the kind of government that hangs betrayers and uses really sharp whips. Then, eh. Not so much. Then Peter would deny he knew Jesus, *even while Jesus was being beaten up.*

When Jesus forgives Peter, we see another example of five-star forgiveness. After Jesus rises from the dead, He has a breakfast cookout with Peter and his friends. Jesus doesn't just forgive Peter; He reconciles him. This means that Jesus not only brings him back into the circle, but He also gives Peter a different path to take, to love better next time, to truly learn the lessons of loyalty and service.

Jesus asks Peter if he loves Him, and when Peter says he does, Jesus tells him, "Feed My sheep." In other words, "Here is your new role, your fresh identity. This is the reconciled, redeemed person you are now."

This is five-star forgiveness you can take to your own life. Jesus forgives you completely, so you can do the same. Forgive completely, forget the betrayal, and move forward to a new, better relationship.

FORGIVENESS STORY 7

That time Jesus forgave the guy next to Him—WHILE HE WAS DYING FOR THE SINS OF THE WORLD (Luke 23:33–46).

★★★★★ for the forgiveness that Jesus gives in the very hardest moments of His life.

Okay, so maybe you are kind of off the hook for this kind of forgiveness because you'll literally never be in a situation where you are on a cross, dying as a sacrifice for the sins of the world.

But we can still look at this forgiveness with total awe. Because what Jesus did really is the ultimate, most impressive display of forgiveness.

Think about this: Just as Jesus is suffering and dying for the sins of all of humankind, the guy next to Him (whom Jesus is dying for so he could have a chance at eternal life, and who is dying himself) starts messing with Him about how He isn't really God. And as the soldiers are gambling to see who gets Jesus' clothes, Jesus asks His Father to forgive all this terrible, mean nonsense that is happening to Him.

This is the amazing love Jesus has for His people. Nothing we do is so bad that it will separate us from His powerful mercy for all of us sinners.

That is more than five-star forgiveness. That's love powerful enough to give us heaven.

GOD'S SILVER (GLITTER) LINING

Even in the Bible, regular people get grace wrong lots of times. But God's forgiveness is the ultimate example of how to love, absolve, and accept those who let you down. Over and over, God's stories are of impossible grace.

You will still get forgiveness wrong lots of times. This means that sometimes you'll have to forgive the same person over and over—sometimes daily—for the same sin.

Other times it will feel like someone absolutely doesn't deserve God's forgiveness. This one person and this one particular sin will just feel like too much to let go.

And other times it will feel so good to carry around your own bitterness. You'll believe that your anger gives you an edge, and you need that so you won't get hurt again. Turning the other cheek and showing grace will feel like really dumb ideas.

These lies might make it hard to forgive, but there's hope. Keep reading the Bible, keep receiving Holy Communion, keep learning more about God's five-star forgiveness. These stories will inspire you and remind you that you are loved with the very best kind of grace, by a God who always welcomes you home.

CONVERSATION SPARKS

1. Rate your own ability to forgive others. Explain your rating. Are you someone who holds grudges and who struggles to show grace? Why or why not?

2. What's another Bible story about forgiveness? Tell the story here and then rate the forgiveness on a five-star scale.

3. Look at 2 Corinthians 12:9. What does this teach us
    about God's grace?

SHINE ON!

Heavenly Father, Your forgiveness is beyond our ability to understand.
Your grace is the perfect gift—so complete and so generous. Thank
You for showing us Your flawless love. Help us, Lord, to love better.
Make us bright lights of Your grace in the darkest parts of the world.
In Jesus' name. Amen.

Keep Calm and Shine On

The LORD bless you and keep you; the LORD make His face to shine upon you and be gracious to you; the LORD lift up His countenance upon you and give you peace.

—NUMBERS 6:24–26

Here we are, near the end of this book, and I still have so much I want you to know. I feel like you're preparing to drive off and I'm leaning in your car window, yelling reminders while you slowly start to pull away.

You've probably already been on the receiving end of lots of moments like this—someone *needs* you to understand the right way to do life, the best advice for living out your faith, and to "Save your money! . . . Do your homework! . . . Get into the best college!"

During these years, you might feel like everyone has a shrill message for you. This might also be when you start to tune out what they're saying. To be honest, I can't blame you. This is your life, and you will probably have to make your own mistakes to learn some of these lessons. Without your own experience, a warning can feel like an empty threat.

So, I have a better way to close this book. Let me leave you with the ancient blessing God gave to His people. It's from Numbers 6, and you've probably heard it lots of times, maybe even every week at church. This is a blessing from Aaron, and it's one the priests would give the people before they went into the hard world. It's not filled with frantic warnings, but with love and the best eternal blessings from your God.

"The LORD bless you and keep you." (May God fill your life with the blessings of faith, forgiveness, and your strong security in Him. May He keep you with Him—the only good place to be.)

"The LORD make His face to shine upon you and be gracious to you." (May He cover you with His glowing love, so you can be like a solar panel, storing up His goodness and sharing it with the world. May He be gracious to replenish your sparkle every day and redeem your mistakes for His glory.)

"The LORD lift up His countenance upon you." (May your heavenly Father shine His dazzling, brilliant love so you can tell the world that there is hope in Jesus, that there is more than just this flimsy life on earth.)

And finally, may the Lord "give you peace." (Because, yes, the hard, dark parts of life will probably be harder and darker than you want. But you belong to the Lord, dear girl, and because of that, you can have deep peace. You can weather the darkness.)

Carry that peace in your smile, in your words, and in your spirit forever.

Keep calm—your soul full of God's peace—and shine on.

Moody and Bitter

(Why You Shouldn't Let Other People's Reactions Decide Who You Are)

Here's a universal truth we all seem to accept: the way people react to you tells you who you are. Your whole worth can feel wrapped up in whether or not those around you are happy with you. It's like one of those exercise trackers you wear on your wrist that tells how many steps you've taken—except you're looking for smiles instead of miles. "Twelve smiles, two dozen Instagram 'likes,' and three compliments—and it's not even noon. I am so worthy."

There's a dark side to this mind-set, though. If everyone, from your parents to your neighbors to the barista to the cute boy in math class, seems bitter around you, this might feel like it's about you too. Tying your worth to how people react to you is tricky because sometimes (most times?) they don't seem happy at all. And what does that say about you?

Here's why it's a terrible idea to take the world's reactions personally:

1. EVERYONE IS SO MOODY.

Okay, this isn't exactly headline news. Of course everyone is moody. You probably know this is true because you also feel like you're living in the emotional space of some kind of Pirates Plunge Roller Coaster.

You know that scene in *Inside Out* when Sadness grabs control of Riley's life and then Joy grabs the controls and Riley feels like a hot mess? Yes, this is exactly right.

One day the world is bright with Technicolor possibility. An F on a test? No problem because you will just try harder next time!

Hair that looks like a rodent made a (greasy) nest in it? Dry shampoo and a high ponytail . . . done!

Mom is out of town and you have to make your own meals and get yourself to school? What a fun challenge. No problem for you because you have got this.

But then . . . the dramatic emotional plunge, and everything shifts. Nothing seems easy, and the world is only a gloomy existence where you are too young or too old and all of your clothes make you look like a clown who ate too many Twinkies.

Now you can see the world for how difficult it really is. Your parents are SO on your last nerve that you're considering a Countdown Until I Move Out calendar to paint on the kitchen wall.

Your favorite English teacher was having a down day when she graded your essay, and she wrote comments like "This is a sentence fragment! You should know better by now!" and it feels like an act of personal aggression.

Plus, your sweet grandma is in a bad mood, and she jabs you with her elbow during church for blowing your nose too loudly. She glares at you with such a death stare, you are sure you just got kicked out of her will for having allergies.

You see now that you can't really trust any of your friends because they are gossipy and shallow and more worried about themselves than you.

School is a joke with tyrannical teachers and stupid rules. Your cat is the only one who really loves you—and she just threw up on your bed. Awesome.

What's the problem with this?

The problem comes when you decide you are a worthy person only when other people are happy with you.

Pretty soon you discover that everyone else is also going through this same roller coaster of emotions. So if you ask your sister for a ride to practice on Monday, she'll smile and tell you to hop into the car and that you get to pick the radio station.

But if you ask on Wednesday? Get ready for World War III, including a long lecture on how "you are so selfish and treat your family like your personal Uber." What changed? Probably just her mood.

It's true that moods are about as stable as the weather. When it rains on your birthday, you don't take that personally. Why would you? That's arbitrary and says nothing about who you are.

Could you do the same with the moods of the people around you?

2. EVERYONE IS CARRYING SO MUCH BAGGAGE.

Imagine your suitcase from the last trip you took. You brought pjs and underwear, all your toiletries, makeup, and your magical hair tools that transform your crazy curls into a sleek style.

You filled your suitcase with outfits for whatever you had planned on vacation: beach time, dinners in restaurants, hanging out before bed, touristy days, and the long hours back in the car or on the plane. You tucked your phone charger, earbuds, snacks, and extra jacket into your backpack.

Then you zipped up that bag. For the next week or so, it was your responsibility to carry everything in there around with you. You held on to it through the busy airport, while standing in the long security line, and on the tour bus. This was the stuff that would keep you comfortable and safe.

You also pack up an emotional suitcase, filled with the experiences that have happened to you. You feel like it's your responsibility to carry all of this with you everywhere. These memories and feelings are in your subconscious and they become your identity, the way you treat other people, and how you see the world.

You carry around the people who have really hurt you or even abused you. You also lug around the feelings from those who have loved you well and who have taken very good care of you. You clutch these memories in hopes that you will find someone who will love you like that again. You won't let yourself forget those who were mean to you, because you need to avoid others like this in the future. It's your responsibility to hold on to all of this baggage.

It's with this emotional luggage—these memories and fears and hurts and hopes—that you react to the world.

What's the problem with this?

You can't really know what emotional baggage other people are lugging. It's so personal that you might not even understand what's in the suitcase of your very best friend, of your mom, or even of your sister.

But you can be sure that each of them is carrying what they think they need to survive. "Don't forget your toothbrush!" becomes "Don't forget that people who talk about God are dangerous" for some people.

Or "Don't forget that every single boy wants to hurt you." Or "If you want to stay safe, you must look adorable every single second of your life. Never let anyone know how ugly you believe you really are."

The problem comes when you try to mess with the baggage another person is carrying. They will react so dramatically and suddenly that you will be left believing that you did something horribly wrong. You'll feel like an insensitive person who deserves their reaction.

When you tell your mom you're going to a concert and she freaks out, you'll never know that she's thinking about the girl in her high school who was abducted at a concert thirty years ago. Your mom might not even remember that's exactly the memory packed in her emotional suitcase, but she knows she doesn't like kids at concerts. Pretty soon, you're having a big argument and you can only decide that your mom doesn't trust you because of something stupid you've done.

Or think about your friend who has been freaking out about you not taking care of yourself. It's true that your leg has been hurting and that she keeps telling you that you must go to the doctor. You start to believe her and worry that maybe you are really bad at health stuff and that you'll probably end up with some chronic illness because you can't even get yourself to the doctor for a pain in your shin.

But how could you know that the memories this particular friend has packed in her suitcase are of her grandma who had a brain tumor no one knew about? Your friend's fear and warnings have everything to do with that, and really nothing to do with you or how good you are at scheduling an x-ray for yourself.

3. DON'T TAKE IT PERSONALLY

This can be tricky because so much of how we interact with the world has to do with the emotional luggage we are lugging around. So many confrontations with others, from the one with your angry brother to the one with the grouchy woman in the school office who gives you tardies, are coming from their own emotional baggage.

It can be helpful to remember the emotional suitcase when someone reacts really strongly to you. When you forget to text a new friend back and she gives you the silent treatment the next day, you might be poking around in what she has packed in her emotional suitcase to keep herself comfortable in relationships. You've just jabbed "Trust no one because they will hurt you."

Or you'll be talking to your crush, and he'll suddenly get bitter about the teacher who yelled at him. Like, really bitter. You might be rooting around in the way that he's been yelled at by his angry dad.

But could you remember that this probably has very little to do with you? Could you see that it's not that you are a TERRIBLE TEXTER, as your new friend would want you to believe, but that she is carrying this fear in her own suitcase and taking it out on you?

GOD'S SILVER (GLITTER) LINING

Again, everyone is moody and is carrying around so much of their own baggage that you can't believe these lies: "If people smile at me, if boys tell me I'm cute, and if strangers and my parents think I'm the very most helpful and sweet girl in the world, then I will know for sure that God loves me too."

This is the exact *opposite* message of what God wants you to know. He has already chosen you in your Baptism. You are already worthy because of what Jesus did on the cross. The approval or bad moods or praise or criticism from people has nothing to do with that.

Check out God's promises in Ephesians 1:3–4:

Blessed be the God and Father of our Lord Jesus Christ, who has blessed us in Christ with every spiritual blessing in the heavenly places, even as He chose us in Him before the foundation of the world, that we should be holy and blameless before Him.

The writer of this, Paul, is so excited to tell us this Good News that he writes it all in one long, run-on sentence. Think of your little sister when she comes home from kindergarten and wants to tell you ALL THE THINGS. That's Paul here. He can't even stop for a breath because this is just too important, too exciting, too good.

You are deeply loved and so worthy. Because of that, God has given you all the important blessings (forgiveness of sins, eternity with Him, deep peace, acceptance, and His unconditional love). The work was done when Jesus died on the cross. You are the cherished, adopted daughter whom God chose.

So when you bump up against the bad moods and the baggage of other people, you can reflect God's love to them. You can share with them the message that they are fully loved and accepted and celebrated because of what Jesus did on the cross.

CONVERSATION SPARKS

1. Talk about what you've learned about moodiness and other people's baggage. When have you found yourself defining yourself by other people's bad moods and emotional baggage?

2. Some versions of Numbers 6:24–26 include the phrase "May God smile upon you." Talk about this wording. How can this be a good reminder as a blessing for each of us?

3. How can you react the next time you find yourself in the crosshairs of someone else's bad mood or emotional baggage? Name a couple of strategies for remembering you are worthy because of Jesus' love for you.

SHINE ON!

Thank You, heavenly Father, for blessing me with Your peace, with Your shining face, and with Your constant care. Please help me to know You always love me. Remind me of my worth through Jesus. Help me to sparkle Your love to those who are struggling with their own darkness. In the name of Your Son. Amen.

Find Your Best Recharge Strategy

(A Quiz about How You Can Stay Connected to Your Savior)

Yes, girl, you are so ready to shine. You are fully equipped to sparkle our Lord's love everywhere. Your Father has given you His peace, His love, and His smile to spread like bright glitter everywhere you go.

But as you probably know, you will sometimes feel empty, tired, and insecure. Even though you know who you are, you will sometimes feel like you don't have anything bright to share.

What's the best way for you to stay connected to your Savior, to recharge your faith, so you can spread the Good News to those who need it?

Take this quiz to find out your preferred type of recharging.

1. Vaping Violation

Vaping is huge at your high school, and you have promised your parents you'll never try it. But now your best friend is vaping, and it's hard because everyone is putting so much pressure on you to just try one little hit.

You need to stay strong in your promise to your mom and dad. You think that prayer would help you here.

Which of these would help you most to remember to pray?

> A. Is there an app for praying? Because I could remember to pray for strength if I had a little alarm dinging every couple of hours and reminding me. I'm on my phone anyway, and this would tell me that God can help me deal with the whole everyone-is-constantly-vaping-in-the-bathroom problem happening at my high school.

B. I need a friend here, for sure. Obviously I don't need the kind of friend who wants me to meet her in the bathroom to inhale a little of the mango-flavored vapor. No, I need someone I can trust and who will pray with me. Nothing keeps me accountable like the friend I don't want to let down.

C. A prayer journal would really help me. I need someplace private where I can tell God what I really think about vaping, and how my friends are pressuring me to try it, and about how I haven't told my parents that everyone is doing it, and it's so hard to keep saying no.

2. The Evolution of Your Faith

This year you're in AP biology class, and it's all pretty amazing and also a little awkward. The teacher has a PhD in evolutionary science, and he seems to know everything about dinosaurs, how humans have evolved over the past million years, and what it means that there are ocean fossils. Also, he really hates the idea of God and six-day creation. Like it's this guy's personal mission to erase Adam and Eve and the Garden of Eden from your life. You need some help understanding Genesis so you can defend what you believe.

Where would you turn for help?

A. The smartest Christians in the world have written so much about exactly this. Visit websites like The Creation Museum, Museum of the Bible, and Answers in Genesis for help. Download the interactive apps that explain the intersection of faith and science. Use these to understand your faith–and explain it to anyone else who wants to understand both evolution and creation.

B. Find someone who understands all the arguments and truth about creation and the Big Bang Theory and also believes that God uses intelligent design to care for His creation. Email this expert and ask all your questions. Also, check in with your pastor about resources he has to help you.

C. Go to your friendly local library and check out every book you can about this. Read and make notes until you really get the two sides of the discussion. Come prepared for the next time your teacher starts ranting that creation is a fairy tale.

3. Gather in God's Name

Your parents have never been great about getting to church, and now that your family has moved to a new city, they're really bad about it. They say they need to find a church, but they haven't even started looking. You know you need church, and you also think your little sister could use it. It looks like it's up to you two to find someplace to worship.

How do you find a church?

A. The internet is like a tour of all the churches in your new neighborhood. Read all the websites for mission statements, youth programs, and service times. Even read reviews from people who love the music at this church and the pastor's sermons at that one. When you have three good options, pack up your sister and call a Sunday morning Uber.

B. Poll your friends about where they go to church. Invite yourself to the next youth event and meet everyone. Tell the youth director your situation and ask her to let you know about whatever they're doing.

C.   Church is a superpersonal preference, and so you head out and visit them. Sometimes your little sister comes along, sometimes your mom does, and sometimes you (awkwardly) go by yourself. It's fine, though. It's easiest for you to think about what you like best when you can dive deep into your own thoughts and experience church from your own head.

4. Devote Daily

Suddenly you're living a life straight out of *Greenhouse Academy*. You broke up with your boyfriend, and now he's texting your best friend. You were hired at your favorite escape room, and then it immediately went out of business. And your dad just announced he's taking a new job on the other side of the country, so he's renting an apartment thousands of miles from home.

All these changes are so confusing that it's hard to know what good is happening and what's falling apart. You need a compass here. You need something to help you know what God wants you to do with all the drama in your life.

You need a devotion—like, every day.

A.   Podcasts! Daily texts from your favorite Bible app! An email from your favorite Christian vlogger with his daily devotion. All of these will help keep you on track so you can hear God's voice above the craziness that is your current life.

B.   You call your friend and announce that the two of you are meeting every day for Bible study. When she complains about not having time, you tell her it will be a ten-minute FaceTime where you read the Bible together. She's hesitant to commit but only because she will take this so seriously. As soon as you have her on board, you know this will happen.

C. You buy the best daily devotion book you can find and make an appointment with yourself every day to read it and write a sentence or two about what this means to you.

5. Wash the Feet and Wash the Cars

So much bugs you about the unfairness of the world. Mostly because you feel guilty about all the comforts you have that other people don't. Your family is great, and you have a nice warm house, a good school, and plenty of money to get what you need.

You want to help the people who don't have what they need right now. If Jesus can wash feet, you could surely find a way to get shoes for the homeless—or at least visit your grandma in her nursing home.

How can you help out?

A. Your neighbors want to set up a GoFundMe to buy a handicapped-accessible van for their daughter with cerebral palsy. You help them with the website and spread the word on all your social media accounts.

B. The friends who serve together, stay together. Actually, that's probably not a real saying, but it should be. Because there is nothing more fun than getting your girls together for a lemonade stand in the park or a Christ Critter Camp to teach the kids in your neighborhood about animals and about how much Jesus loves them.

C. When you heard about the water crisis in Africa, you knew you needed to help. By writing more than a hundred letters, you'll start a campaign to get the word out about how villages need clean drinking water. You'll follow up with all these people and then send out more information to help fund a well in a rural part of Uganda.

6. Go and Make Disciples (in Your Chemistry Class)

Your new friend in chemistry class is Muslim. You bond over chemical equations and studying for the killer midterm. You talk for hours about your teachers, your finals, your lives—and eventually, your faith. She explains her family's tradition, and she also shares her struggles with what they believe. She asks you so many questions about Jesus and Baptism that you know she's interested in what all this would mean for her. What are the best ways to share your faith?

A. Why try to explain what you believe when there are actual videos of the best-ever speakers explaining it? Show her a couple of YouTube videos of The Skit Guys explaining Baptism and of your favorite online preacher telling who Jesus is. When your friend is interested, find more and more of the best videos about Christianity and text them to her.

B. Just go ahead and invite your friend to Advent services at your church. Tell her that the old ladies in your church make the most delicious soup and the service is really pretty, with lots of your favorite songs. Afterward, get coffee together and answer any questions she has about baby Jesus and what it means that He came to earth to die for our sins.

C. You write your own personal testimony, practice it several times, and then share it with your friend. Tell her what Baptism means to you and the ways your faith is different from hers. When she asks questions about why Jesus had to die on the cross, answer the best that you can, and then go back to your computer and draft a deeper answer to her question that references Bible verses.

IF YOU ANSWERED MOSTLY A'S . . .

You like tools—especially techie tools—to help recharge your faith. The best way for you to keep connected to God is through your phone, your computer screen, or any other way you can get to the internet and all the wonderful gizmos that make life as a Christian in the twenty-first century easier.

IF YOU ANSWERED MOSTLY B'S . . .

For you, connecting with other people strengthens your faith. Church, Bible studies, service, and devotions are so much more fun when you're doing them with a friend. Plus, other people keep you accountable to help you make it to church and the events.

IF YOU ANSWERED MOSTLY C'S . . .

Worship and prayer and Bible study are very personal for you. You think best when you're deep in your own thoughts. For you, growing in your faith happens in your heart, and then you're ready to share that with the world.

GOD'S SILVER (GLITTER) LINING

Isn't it kind of amazing how God has made each of us so different? I mean, seriously, God's creativity puts the best Pinterest projects to shame. He created you to be an extrovert who feels most recharged when you're with friends. Your sister might be an introvert who makes sense of the world deep in her own head. He also gives us all these creative tools, including apps and videos and podcasts and

His Word and friends and youth leaders and encouraging friends. Just, wow.

Our world is filled with endless ways to stay in God's Word. This is your encouragement to find your best strategy and to keep connecting with your heavenly Father.

Your soul is like that solar panel, storing up God's love, ready to share it with the world. Recharge often with prayer, Scripture, and time with your heavenly Father.

CONVERSATION SPARKS

1. Discuss your quiz answers. Overall, how do you best recharge? Talk about these as a part of your daily schedule. In what ways do you incorporate these habits into your day?

2. Read Colossians 1:3-14. What is Paul's encouragement to believers about staying strong in their faith? Talk about how this relates to what you've learned about yourself and your best habits for staying connected to Jesus.

3. In your own words, what role does the Holy Spirit play in your faith life? Tell how your faith is created and then the ways it grows.

SHINE ON!

Heavenly Father, thank You for all the ways You take care of me. Help me to stay connected to Your love every moment of every day. Recharge Your Spirit in my soul so I can share Your grace with the world. Help me to love well, dear Jesus. In Your name. Amen.

The Darkness and the Hope

In my life, I've struggled with real hope-crushing sadness. Not just the kind of sadness that comes from something hard that's happened, but the kind that shifts my whole outlook on life.

My worst season of darkness came when I started middle school. The Disney Channel could have made a show about me as The Girl Most Poorly Prepared for the Seventh Grade.

Imagine a large, bald ostrich, with its weird pink skin and awkward long neck and skinny legs. With my thin blonde hair and bony legs, I was that ostrich at Weis Middle School. I bobbed through the halls between these clusters of beautiful red and yellow birds.

Not only was I an ostrich, but I was surrounded by poachers who needed to punish me for looking so weird. They tripped me, made nasty noises, put ketchup packets on my chair, and called me names that were so R-rated, my private-schooled self didn't even understand them.

When I visited the school counselor, she told me I needed to get thicker skin. I think maybe there was some truth in that, but it wasn't very helpful as a coping strategy. I tried everything: laughing along with the bullies, pretending to be sick, telling the teacher, and finally, walking out of the classroom to go home and give up.

I barely survived the year. Every day was hard. My stomach hurt constantly, and I cried a lot. I was so ashamed that I looked different and didn't get the jokes and couldn't make friends, but I was also ashamed about how sad I was.

Up until then, I had been such a happy kid. I really wanted to make my parents, teachers, and classmates happy, but I was letting everyone down. I couldn't see a success plan here. In this new place, I couldn't be the easygoing, sweet girl I had been before. I just didn't fit in, and that was failure. All of it felt physically painful.

Seventh grade eventually got better for me. The teachers paid more attention to the trouble I was having, the kids found someone else to pick on, I made some nice friends, and I stopped caring (a little bit) about my own awkwardness. I had some wonderful moments of prayer. For the first time, I really knew that God was active in my life.

Even though that year still sticks out as the worst for me, I also learned a lot from the experience. Most of all, I learned about hope. Because that school counselor was a little bit right about my thin skin. I had no coping strategies for the hard parts of life. When the teasing started, I didn't understand that it wouldn't last forever. I had no perspective that their bullying didn't define me. Everything felt so hopeless.

Here's what I wish I could tell my seventh-grade self: "You, sweet girl, are going to be okay. Yes, you're dealing with a lot right now. Yes, it hurts, and I understand how much you hate all of this. But it will get better. You will have a whole life of moments so beautiful, they'll take your breath away. You can't see it now, but one day God will redeem all this pain. You'll be a teacher, and you'll tell your students that you truly do understand how much it hurts to not fit in. You'll remind the outcasts not to let the mean kids define them. You'll be a mom to sensitive sons and daughters, and they'll need to hear the lessons you learned in those horrible middle school hallways. Most of all, that hard season will teach you about hope. Because even when it seems like there's no hope, God is doing something bigger. I promise. You can count on this more than anything else. This season will end up being about you trusting God, and that lesson will get you through other really hard seasons in your life. So hold on, dear one. You're going to be okay. Better, actually."

GOD'S SILVER (GLITTER) LINING

There is a '90s movie called *Hope Floats* about a woman who goes through all the worst drama you can imagine (divorce, death, grief, embarrassment, and financial ruin). In the movie, she has to put her life together, even though it seems hopeless. She finally finds hope in a romance with a cute guy who takes her fishing and line dancing. It's called *Hope Floats* because hope gets her through. In the movie, it's the cute guy that gives her hope.

But as you've probably learned, cute guys and movies don't really provide the hope we need. I mean, both can be *really* fun distractions, but we need something deeper to believe in, a true hope.

There is only one true hope that will save us and that is Jesus. We will find so many fun distractions (the search for the right college, the best grades, the promising political candidate, the grand adventure—and yes, the fun romance).

But it's our Savior who will give us the real peace. He provides the hope because He really does know us and love us. You can trust this. It's the promise that puts the sparkle in our lives—and fills even the hardest seasons with hope.

CONVERSATION SPARKS

1. Tell about a season of darkness you've survived. What felt hopeless? What deeper hope did you have?

2. Talk about the difference between earthly hope and heavenly hope. How has God given us real hope through His Son, Jesus?

3. Read 1 Peter 5:10. What does this say about suffering and God's help in our lives? How does this give you hope?

SHINE ON!

Dear Jesus, thank You for living a perfect life and dying on the cross for my sins. Be with me when I feel hopeless. Show me the deeper love through each of my hardest seasons. Give me Your peace and help me to share it with those in darkness. In Your name. Amen.

Five Best and Five Worst Bits of Advice

Most of the time, people who have advice for you also have an ulterior motive. Your aunt wants you to get good grades because she wants you to go to the college where she teaches. Your dad is filled with advice about how to pitch because he wants you to continue his legacy as The King of Strikeouts. Your older brother downloads wisdom to you constantly because he really wants to make sure you don't make the same mistakes he made.

Some of the advice you hear will be good, Bible based, and helpful. Other times, you'll get a whole lot of bad opinions from those who want to sell you something or who have a weird view of what will make you happy.

Let's talk about what can really help you live your best, most glitter-filled, brilliant life—and what will not help.

IF YOU WANT TO SPARKLE FOR YOUR SAVIOR, HERE IS THE BEST ADVICE

1. Fangirl yourself.

Please know that you are God's child, and because of that, you are incredibly valuable.

This means it's okay to take very good care of yourself. Become your biggest fangirl. Serve yourself like a flight attendant would. "Can I get you anything? How is this trip going for you? What do you need for the next part of the journey (this day, this difficult time, this semester, this year)?"

This also means you have to say no to the terrible habit of bullying yourself. Don't mutter, "You are such an idiot. You are so fat. You don't deserve that. You are so bad at this." If you're already in the habit of this, just stop it.

Instead, hear that God calls you His daughter (Romans 8:14; it is understood that daughters are equally included when the Bible speaks here of "sons" [ESV]); "beautiful" (Song of Solomon 4:7); "consecrated" (Jeremiah 1:5), which means "chosen"; "loved" (Ephesians 2:4); "wonderfully made" (Psalm 139:14); and "precious" (1 Peter 1:7).

2. For making decisions, God is not as subtle as you probably think.

When faced with two options, choose the one that honors God the most.

How are you supposed to know which one honors God? Get to know Him by reading what He wrote to you in your Bible.

Then ask yourself these questions: Which choice will show people that Jesus loves them? Which option will give you the time and opportunities to go back to your Master Teacher every day for more love and instruction? Which decision shows the most obedience to God and His commandments? Which route trusts that God will love you and take care of you?

3. Everyone is doing their best, even when it doesn't look like it.

In the moment when your friends or parents are letting you down, it will not feel like they are trying very hard at all. It will feel very personal when they yell at you or forget you or hurt you. You will think that they are all very bad at being parents and friends.

It's not personal, and they are not bad at loving you. Okay, sometimes they are, but they don't mean to be.

Everyone is doing their very best—and they still will let you down. Humans are just so infected with this sin. It makes us selfish, mean, greedy, and bitter.

Give them grace. They are trying to love better, but they need a Savior.

The Good News is they have one.

4. Never, ever give up on God.

Most Christians who have seen some real hard life (death, disease, disappointment) will tell you that God never lets you down. Ever. Your Father is taking perfect care of you—in the most creative and complete ways. This will sometimes be hard for you to see, but it's still the true Good News.

God's timing will be different from what you expect. He will provide a way out, even when it's not the way you had guessed. The Holy Spirit will always give you the meaningful joy, the better peace, the very best security.

You will walk through seasons where it will feel like God has abandoned you. He has not. Keep your faith in God and your eye on Jesus' love for you. Your heavenly Father will give you richer blessings and better timing than you could have ever hoped.

5. Make friends with your fear.

The world really wants you to conquer your fears. It's practically the mantra of every advertising campaign: This Product Will Make You Braver!

It can feel like fear is your enemy. "If only I wasn't so scared, I could really accomplish my goals."

Fear can be your friend, though. It's what warns you about picking up a snake or talking to the creepy guy in the white van. Fear is part of being human, and the opposite of fear isn't courage. It's faith.

Trusting God is different from having courage because it's not about trying to overcome your fear—it's handing it to your Savior. This involves listening to His Word and telling Him about your fears. This is about trusting that God's ways are the best ways.

You can make friends with your fear. You can say to it, "Yes, I hear you, fear. Yes, you are helpful in keeping me alive and out of trouble. Thank you. But you are not in charge of my life. God is. I will be trusting Him."

So do that. Take God at His Word when He promises He'll be with you for every single breath. He loves you, and His protection is as close as the skin on your face.

IF YOU WANT TO SPARKLE FOR YOUR SAVIOR, HERE IS THE WORST ADVICE

1. These are the best years of your life.

The movie and advertising industries have conspired to convince teens that this decade is the very best season of your life. But actually, this is a terrible lie to believe.

Because what hope is there if your best years are already over when you're only 20 percent into your life?

If this were a meal, this would mean that right after the appetizer, everyone at the table would announce, "Well, that was the only good food we'll have. The soup, salad, and main course will be a huge letdown. Brace yourself for a real disappointment of a meal. Even when you're eating from the chef's special dessert menu, you'll still be fantasizing about how tasty that calamari at the start was."

No, this is ridiculous. There is no season of your life that is any better than any other season. They're all filled with their own adventures, grief, disappointments, brilliant joy, and lessons. God is transforming you all the time. He's teaching you and growing you, and that's a lifetime adventure—not one that ends on your twentieth birthday.

2. You're doing it wrong.

One of the biggest lies you'll hear over the next few years is that there is one way to do everything, and if life feels hard, then you must be doing it wrong.

You don't know the right way to be a friend. You're the wrong kind of daughter. This is not the way you're supposed to do high school. You're struggling because you care too much. You're hurting because you don't care enough. Also, you're too introverted, too extroverted, too quiet, or way too loud.

The truth is that life is hard. You're struggling to make friends, you're getting your feelings hurt, and you're frustrated by your family because this is part of the human experience. It's full of sin and ego and mistakes, and a lot of this grief cannot be controlled or avoided.

The good news is that God doesn't abandon you in the human experience. He even sent His Son to earth to live it—and to show all of us what a life of perfect love for us looks like.

3. You are (almost) perfect.

You are (almost) the perfect girlfriend, if you would just have sex with me.

You are (almost) the perfect friend, but you must do exactly what I say.

You are (almost) the perfect selfie, but you just need this outfit/hair straightener/to lose five pounds.

You are (almost) the perfect student; you just need to score a few more points on the ACT/earn more A's/study harder.

You are (almost) the perfect daughter, if you would just keep your room cleaner/get a job/unload the dishwasher without being told.

This side of heaven, nothing is perfect, almost perfect, or really close to perfect. Don't listen to the people who tell you that if you do exactly what they need you to do, you can finally be accepted.

Everyone has an agenda. Learn this lesson quickly, dear girl, so you can spot this terrible advice when someone tells you that you need to try a little harder to make them happy.

Because you will, in fact, be trying forever—and still never be enough.

Instead, listen to the hundreds of Bible verses and hear the lessons from your heavenly Father.

He says you already are enough and that He loves you completely.

4. There is no one in the world who has ever struggled like you.

Yes, you are wonderfully unique. Of course God created you to have your own experiences, talents, passions, and dreams.

And yet, you are also just like everyone else who has ever lived and who ever will live.

The world will convince you that you cannot possibly be expected to overcome your unique burdens. Because of your highly complicated and difficult personality, you will find it much harder than anyone else to ever be happy/successful/kind/peaceful. You should have a chip on your shoulder for the struggles you've had to endure. It's not fair, and you are a victim.

This might feel true, but it is not.

The truth is that billions of people have struggles, and we all also have hope. Or as God tells us, we all need a Savior (because our struggle is sin) and we all have Jesus (because our hope is in Him alone).

In other words, you are flawed in exactly the same way everyone else is flawed. You really like being in charge of your own life. You believe your opinions and experiences are the right ones. You trust the wrong people and worship the wrong things. You feel unloved and then don't show love like you know you should. You're full of your own unique troubles—and so is everyone else.

You need a Savior. All people, from the Dalai Lama to Drake to your grandma, are looking for something to save them. We all have this nagging hole in our soul. We will try to fill it with nearly everything else. But really, we need Jesus.

The good news is that Jesus is pursuing us all the time. And He is our Savior. He loves you so individually that He even knows how many hairs are on your head (Luke 12:7).

So you don't have to believe the lie that you are a victim of struggles so unique that you can never, ever conquer them. Jesus has already done the work on the cross, and that victory is yours too.

5. "You cannot handle the truth."

How often do you hear this one—that kids can't handle the truth of this world? So many well-intentioned adults want to protect you from the ugliest political drama, from the ways the people around you are sinning, and from the terrible evils in this world.

"Little girl, it's better for you to not know what's really going on. What would happen if you knew the truth about what happened to Grandpa or what the adults are worried about? Would you rebel? leave us? quit the church?

"To protect you, we will avoid uncomfortable topics. We won't stress you out with the things that keep us up at night. We absolutely won't mention abortion or mass shootings or our family's history of alcoholism. We don't even know how to deal with all of this, so how would you?"

Here's the truth: most teens know what worries their parents. You know what your mom and dad fight about and what headlines are stressing out all the adults.

But when no one is talking about the scariest parts of life, they seem a million times *scarier*. If the seeds you plant are secrets and fear, that's what you'll grow too.

And so, don't be afraid to talk to your parents about what's going on in your life. Tell them that you have faith that God is in control of this world—and the next. He will bless you with peace, and His countenance will shine on you. With the promise of that, no election, family drama, or bad news can ruin us.

We have an actual Savior, and that means we can keep calm and shine on.

GOD'S SILVER (GLITTER) LINING

Here's the best bit of advice for reflecting God's love to the world: stay connected to Him. Seriously. You are just a branch, but God is the life source. He is the vine (John 15:5).

Your faith will make all the difference. When faith lives in your heart, you'll turn to God when you're afraid, when you're thankful, when you're mad, and when you're in awe of what He's done in your life.

This faith becomes the guiding light for everything. This is the beautiful, brilliant love that you're reflecting to the world.

This is the blessing I leave with you—for God's face to shine upon you and for the Lord to be gracious to you. May the Lord forever keep you in His perfect care.

May you—forever—have faith in that.

CONVERSATION SPARKS

1. Which of these pieces of advice have you heard? Which advice strikes you as a good idea? What advice would you give to girls younger than you?

2. Talk about the advice you hear when you're a teenager. Why should you be careful about the advice you follow? How can you recognize what are good suggestions and which are not?

3. Through our faith, God gives us so many blessings: forgiveness (Luke 7:48), love (John 15:9), eternal life (1 John 5:12), and joy (John 15:11). List the blessings that God promises in Numbers 6:24-26.

SHINE ON!

Heavenly Father, thank You so much for giving me so many ways to stay connected to You. Thank You for sending Jesus, for giving me Your Word, and for taking perfect care of me, dear Lord. Thank You for giving me Your Word that's filled with the very best advice in the world. Guide me in Your ways and help me shine to glorify You, Lord. In Jesus' name. Amen.

Answers

~~~~~~

How to Keep Shining God's Light

1. Answers will vary.

2. We are God's chosen ones, holy and beloved. He has given us compassionate hearts, kindness, humility, meekness, and patience. God's Word shows us examples of forgiveness and tells us about our Savior's perfect forgiveness for us. Through God's Word, we can see the qualities of a Christian friend and how to reflect His love to those He has put in our lives.

3. Answers will vary but will include the individual ways that God provides training and experiences for each of us to help us reflect His love to the world.

One Friday Morning in Santa Fe, Texas . . .

1. Answers will vary.

2. Answers will vary but will include that God is all powerful, all knowing, and all capable. Your heavenly Father is always strengthening your faith and showing you how to rely on Him. Trust that this is the place you want to be, for eternity.

3. Answers will vary but will include that God's desire is for all of His children to spend eternity with Him. The fear and insecurity of this world—which seems so dark and tragic—is nothing compared to the hope we have in Jesus.

Timeline of a Crush

1. Answers will vary.

2. Answers will vary but will include that God wants us to remember that He is our first love. Even though boyfriends can be good, He never wants us to believe our self-worth comes from the approval of another person.

3. Answers will vary but will include that trusting God means being okay about not having a boyfriend. You know who you are because God loves you, not because a boy does.

Ten Signs You Might Be Addicted to Social Media

1. Answers will vary.

2. Answers will vary but will include that God cares for you and gives you His Word to encourage you and help you share His love with the world.

3. Answers will vary but will include that God chose you in your Baptism. Worshiping Him and studying His Word remind you of His love.

If You Give a Girl a Mountain(top) Experience

1. Answers will vary.

2. Peter was shocked by the holiness in front of him. Also, he knew he was right in the middle of a significant moment. He didn't want to leave it and risk going back to the ordinary. Most of us would also react with complete awe.

3. The disciples fell facedown, terrified. When humans witness the power and glory of God, they respond with awe. Jesus lovingly touched His disciples, and He told them not to be afraid and to get up. Finally, He led them down from the mountain.

What Do You Want . . . More?

1. Answers will vary.

2. Answers will vary but might include the observation that seeking to know our Savior better might manifest itself in our personal life in various ways, including reading the Bible, attending a Bible study, listening carefully in church, taking Holy Communion, and so forth.

3. Answers will vary but will include that God cares for you and gives you His Word to encourage you and to help you share His love with the world.

Ten Steps to Transform Your Bedroom

1. Answers will vary.

2. Paul reminds us over and over that we are saved because of God's great love for us. It's not because of anything you or I have done, so we can't boast or compare. We are the ones who are receiving the gift.

3. In Ephesians 2, Paul delivered the good news that we are saved through grace, by faith. This is our radical transformation. Next, Paul gives instructions about how to live in God's love—even in a hostile, sinful world. This is the application of the transformation.

Add Glitter to Your Soul

1. Answers will vary. Encourage every girl to find God's love in her chosen verse.

2. Answers will vary but will include that God's Word is living and active, gives faith, is breathed out by God, is good for training, and will encourage us.

3. God also tells us to pray, to worship regularly, to observe a Sabbath, to receive Holy Communion regularly. Our loving Father works through all of these to strengthen our faith.

Four Churches Where You Might Belong

1. Humans who are trying to share the love of Christ often become involved in their own bad plans, selfishness, desires, and egos. This can damage the Church's mission to share the love of God with the world.

2. Answers will vary but will include that God gives us church as a place to meet for worship, to encourage and to teach one another, and to receive forgiveness and care. Church is a gift for believers, and for most it is a place where they belong with other Christians.

3. Answers will vary but will include being kind and patient with other members, talking to guests, showing up for worship and events, volunteering to help lead and teach, and not being part of the sin of gossiping, fighting, or insulting other members of your church.

Desperate Prayers for Those Who Want to Belong

1. Answers will vary but will include that God doesn't always answer our prayers immediately or with what we think we need right now. God answers our prayers with what is best for us for eternity.

2. Each of us has become God's child in our Baptism. We are forever His children.

3. Answers will vary but will include that God tells us how to share His love with a world that's in darkness. God's love changes our perspective.

Southern Sororities, Not Belonging, and the Scars of High School

1. Answers will vary.

2. Answers will vary.

3. Answers will vary.

Seven Lessons You Learn from Bad Boyfriends

1. Answers will vary.

2. An eye "full of light" belongs to the person who sees the world through God's love and acceptance. When you are secure in belonging to God, you live in His light–it's a part of every bit of you. But when you don't– when you see the world through darkness–you see the world through insecurity, neediness, desire, and sin. It clouds your entire perspective–including boys and dating. Jesus tells us to live in His light, through the acceptance we have as God's children.

3. These letters will vary but will include that God's acceptance means everything, for now and always. You do not have to wonder if you are enough; you do not have to obsess about or over boys. You are the beautiful, intentional creation of your heavenly Father. He loves you–and that is enough.

The Flood and the Football Players

1. Training helps us to become better in more ways than just the original goal. Hours of practice teach you sacrifice and dedication. Competing teaches you to handle pressure. Hard work teaches you how to focus on a goal.

2. Answers will vary but will include that God cares for you and gives you His Word to encourage you and help you share His love with the world.

3. Answers will vary but will include that God provides us with His constant love, a promise of eternal life, forgiveness for every sin, peace through His love, and our identity through His Word and Sacraments.

How to Find Your *Thing*

1. Answers will vary.

2. Both true and false. God's desire is that each and every one of His children lives with Him forever in heaven. However, as humans we often want a much more specific plan than just eternity. God is faithful to provide us with faith and tools to keep us in the faith. That's His plan for each of us.

3. Through the stories and the wisdom in the Bible, we can better understand the person of Jesus Christ and the attributes of our Lord. When we better understand God, we know how to live out His will for our lives.

(Fake) Frequently Asked Questions about Serving

1. Answers will vary but will include that most of us are fearful about getting it wrong. Also, it can be uncomfortable to interact with vulnerable strangers. Our sins of selfishness, laziness, and pride are always part of our view as humans.

2. Answers will vary but will include sharing the Word of God, helping others, feeding, clothing, and sheltering those who need it.

3. Answers will vary.

Show Up!

1. Answers will vary but will include that we sometimes don't answer God's call to serve by showing up. Encourage everyone to pray for faith and for God to lead them when it's hard to connect with a hurting person.

2. Jesus showed up over and over. He ate with those living in darkness, who needed to know about God's love. He talked to Samaritans, Pharisees, and those who hated Him. Most important, He taught everyone about His Father, who loved them so much that He had sent His Son to die for them.

3. Answers will vary but will likely include examples of members caring for people by showing up with meals or at funerals or by visiting members in the hospital or by caring for the community with meals through a food pantry or homeless ministry.

Ten Not-So-Easy Steps to Getting Along with Your Siblings

1. Answers will vary but will include that we can forgive because of God's power in us.

2. Jesus says to forgive your brother seventy-seven times. He's making the point that we should forgive over and over and over.

3. Answers will vary but will include that someone who has been abused by a family member needs to hear the message of love. They can forgive, but it will be complicated and difficult. A pastor or Christian counselor can help victims of abuse to learn how to forgive.

Eight (Fake) Bible Verses about Forgiveness You Won't Find in the Bible

1. God tells us that He loves us so much that He sent Jesus so He could forgive our sins. Because of this, we can share His forgiveness with the world, one relationship blunder at a time. If this feels unnatural, it's because it is. It's *super*natural.

2. Jesus taught how limitless grace is. He also gives us real, practical ways to deal with conflict and how to keep forgiving the difficult people in your life.

3. Answers will vary, but girls will share stories about how they better understand God's grace when they see the world through the lens of His forgiveness. Encourage them to memorize other Scripture to shine God's message to the world.

Pinterest Fails and Internet Forgiveness

1. Answers will vary but will include that bitterness and revenge are natural reactions to a sin against us. God's grace helps us to forgive.

2. Jesus' words in John 8:7 ("Let him who is without sin among you be the first to throw a stone at her") remind us that we are all full of sin. Pumped up with pride, we're tempted to point out everyone else's faults, but Jesus reminds us that we're just the same.

3. Jesus calls Himself the "light of the world." This is part of our identity too. Our Savior, who lives in us, shines His light of forgiveness and love into the darkness.

Seven Stories of Forgiveness

1. Answers will vary.

2. Answers will vary but might include the story of God's forgiveness of Adam and Eve in Genesis 3; David and Mephibosheth in 2 Samuel 9; the woman caught in adultery in John 8:1–11; and Jacob and Esau in Genesis 25, 27, 32–33.

3. Paul says that God's grace is sufficient. This means that His grace is always perfect, always five-star, and always an example for how we can love others.

Moody and Bitter

1. Answers will vary but will include examples of how we react to the moodiness and baggage of those around us. Remember that your identity is firm in the love of Christ—no matter how those around you treat you.

2. Answers will vary but will include that God sees Jesus' sacrifice when He looks at us and, because of that, He is pleased with each of us. Even when it seems like the world is not smiling at you, God is because He loves you as His forever daughter.

3. Answers will vary but will include that we can pray and ask God to remind us of our deeper identities in His love. We can ask our heavenly Father to help others with their bad moods and emotional baggage. Finally, we can try to share God's love with anyone who is angry or bitter.

Find Your Best Recharge Strategy

1. Answers will vary.

2. Answers will vary but will include that believers can be encouraged by God's Word and by one another. We can use any of the tools that God gives us to stay strong in our faith.

3. Answers will vary but will include that God begins your faith life at your Baptism. The Holy Spirit works through the Word and the Sacraments to ignite and stoke the fire of your faith.

The Darkness and the Hope

1. Answers will vary.

2. Even though distractions can be helpful to get through a hard time, they are not the ultimate hope we have in Christ.

3. Answers will vary but will include that God will allow you to suffer, but He will always restore you and make you strong and steadfast.

Five Best and Five Worst Bits of Advice

1. Answers will vary.

2. Answers will vary but will include that good advice should always line up with biblical wisdom.

3. God promises to keep us close to Him, to make His face shine upon us, and to be gracious. God promises to lift His countenance upon us, and He will give us His peace.

Acknowledgments

~~~~~~~~~~

Catie . . . so much of this book is taken from your actual life. Thanks for living as a sparkling illumination of God's love. You are the inexpressible and glorious joy in 1 Peter 1:8 and sunshine in my life. (Sorry this still isn't a book dedication.)

Elisabeth . . . of course you were the first one to hear these words. You love books and writing and the whole creative life that goes along with them. Thank you for decorating my desk with notes of encouragement. I needed them all.

Sam . . . if this book is funny at all, it's because I live with you. Thank you for finding the absurd and silly in regular life. Your faith shines brighter because of your bravery. Keep smiling, Sam, and keep shining for Jesus.

Nate . . . thank you for keeping me company for all the months I wrote this book. As my typing fingers clicked away, you told me stories about swim team and third grade. Your confidence is an inspiration to me, Nate, and you make me smile every day.

Mike . . . your selflessness and sacrifice for all of us make you a shining example of God's love. You are the love of my life, and without you, my shine would not be as bright. Thank you for everything you do so I can do what I love to do.

Mom and Dad . . . thanks for being part of our lives every day. You're both role models of faith, sacrifice, faithfulness, and humility—and these have turned out to be exactly what our family needed. We are so glad you live in Texas.

Amanda . . . you are my person, and there is no one in the world I would rather spread glitter with (and other tacky glitter-like things we find on Amazon). Thank you for all of it: the reading, the encouraging, the dreaming, the jokes, and all the hours you put in to share Jesus with women and teens.

My MomTribe . . . thanks for the prayers (Mo), the loyalty (Jen), the advice (Jill), the wisdom (Barb, Janet, and Aunt Katie), the long-distance love (Stacy and Amy), the unconditional love (Marcilee), and the really good cake (Connie).

Hannah . . . thanks for the deep talks, the Bible study, and for geeking out with me about teen lit. You are a special blessing to me. Who else loves both *Gossip Girl* and Jesus?

Ruth . . . thanks for the daily texts, the editing, and all your prayers. Your friendship blesses me every day. You are the actual best. Literally. (Ha. I couldn't resist.)

Peggy . . . another book together! You care so deeply about sharing God's Word with the world, and that shines through everything you do.

Elizabeth and Lindsey . . . you are the BRIGHT, SHINY GLITTER at Concordia Publishing House. Thanks for the video chats; answering all my emails; being your creative, faithful selves; and always giving 173 percent to every project.

Laura Lane . . . thanks for believing in this project and your work to share the message of Jesus' love with teens.

Everyone at CPH . . . for 150 years you have shared God's Word with the world, and I'm so honored to be a tiny part of that work.

Jessica . . . for bravely sharing her story about the mass shooting at Santa Fe High School.

The Avett Brothers and Indigo Girls . . . for your passion, music, and beautiful words. Lyrics get into a writer's head, and therefore your music shines on these pages.

Our kids' teachers . . . who work hard every day to encourage them.

Maria Rodriguez . . . for your faithful help to our family.

Jesus . . . thanks for everything. Literally. I promise to shine for You forever.